AMERICAN NATURE GUIDES
SALTWATER FISH

AMERICAN NATURE GUIDES
SALTWATER FISH

C. RICHARD ROBINS

SMITHMARK

This edition first published by
SMITHMARK Publishers Inc.,
112 Madison Avenue, New York 10016

Published in England by Dragon's World Ltd,
Limpsfield and London

Editor: Diana Steedman
Designer: Carole Perks
Art Director: Dave Allen
Editorial Director: Pippa Rubinstein

SMITHMARK Books are available for bulk purchase for sales
promotions and premium use. For details write or telephone
the Manager of Special Sales, SMITHMARK Publishers Inc.,
112 Madison Avenue, New York, New York 10016.
(212) 532-6600

ISBN 0 8317 6971 8

Printed in Singapore

Contents

Introduction

For our purposes in this nature guide, North America is taken to comprise the continental area north of Mexico from the shoreline – including bays, coastal lagoons, and tidal creeks – to the edge of the Continental Shelf. This area harbors a diverse and rich marine fish fauna which accounts for about eight per cent of the world's fish species, with at least 198 families represented. It has not been possible to include a representative of every family, but those excluded occur either only in the extreme southeastern part of North America (mainly on the coral reef tract along the Florida Keys), or are poorly understood, or are essentially deep water or oceanic groups, with only a few species entering shelf waters.

Distribution of Fishes

Slightly more than six per cent of the 1732 marine fishes occurring in North America are found off both the Atlantic and Pacific Coasts. There are two basic types: **Arctic** species which come southward along Labrador and Newfoundland in the east, and into the Bering Sea (occasionally farther south) in the west; and **pelagic**, **mesopelagic**, and **oceanic** species which have nearly worldwide distributions.

Water temperature, geographic barriers (including the geological history of the area), and ecology define the distribution of most fish families. For example, the sculpins (Cottidae), seasnails (Liparidae), and poachers (Agonidae) are cold-water fishes and are the dominant families in the Gulf of Alaska. Butterflyfishes (Chaetodontidae), angelfishes (Pomacanthidae), parrotfishes (Scaridae), and squirrelfishes (Holocentridae) are warm-water species best represented in the extreme south. Marine representatives of the sturgeons (Acipenseridae), lampreys (Petomyzontidae), and salmons (Salmonidae) all have to migrate to fresh waters to spawn.

Geography and Ecology

The great variety of climate and habitat that are found along the Atlantic and Pacific Coasts provide the conditions necessary to support large numbers of species. The Atlantic and Pacific coastlines differ in their ocean current systems and the tides vary widely. For example, the Atlantic Coast has very small tides in southeastern Florida, while in the Bay of Fundy the tides rank among the highest in the world. Tides also vary from a single cycle per day along parts of the Gulf Coast to the more usual two cycles per day almost everywhere else. The Pacific Coast has a steep profile with a narrow shelf (except in the Bering Sea) whereas along the Atlantic Coast (except southeastern Florida) the Continental Shelf is very broad. The Atlantic shoreline is dominated by estuaries of the "drowned river mouth" type in the northeast and by tidal creeks, lagoons, and salt marshes in the southeastern and Gulf Coast states. On the Pacific Coast, rivers plunge directly into the sea and bays are related to faulting and other geological phenomena.

Atlantic Coast
In the western Atlantic a strong western boundary current, the Gulf Stream, moves warm water northward, and eddies or meanders from the edge of this stream are sometimes isolated as warm core rings which move shoreward from the middle

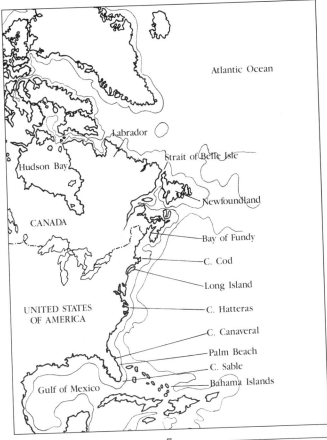

Atlantic states to the banks off southeastern Canada. Many tropical species, especially juveniles, stray during the summer months along the northeastern coasts of the USA and extreme southeastern Canada. In contract, the Arctic waters of the Labrador Current create frigid coastal conditions south to the Strait of Belle Isle between Labrador and Newfoundland and along the outer coast of Newfoundland. Fishes living in these waters live at temperatures below the freezing point of their body fluids, and they must have "antifreeze" adaptations to cope. Not surprisingly southeastern Canada is a mixing ground and nearly half of its 538 species of fishes are strays from the south or the open ocean, many of them in early life-history stages. Although strays confuse the general picture to some extent, the Atlantic fish fauna is latitudinally divisible into tropical, warm temperate, cold temperate, and Arctic elements. In addition to the Strait of Belle Isle, other important faunal boundaries are at Cape Cod, Cape Hatteras, Cape Canaveral, and Cape Sable (at the southern tip of Florida).

In the eastern coastal waters of North America there are some 1127 species, the greatest diversity being in the southeast, especially Florida. Tropical fishes occur primarily along the coral reef tract along the Florida Keys, but many occur elsewhere: in pockets north to Palm Beach, Florida, where the warm Florida Current is closest to shore; in the midshelf bottom waters along the Carolinas; in the northeastern Gulf of Mexico on the Florida Middle Grounds; and in the northwestern Gulf of Mexico at the Flower Garden Reefs of Texas. Tropical fishes, especially their early life-history stages, are carried northward in the Gulf Stream and move onshore in eddies, often far north of their normal range. Where heated effluents occur, as around power plants, small colonies of tropical waifs may survive, though they do not reproduce successfully.

Very few species range from the maritime provinces of eastern Canada all the way to Florida and the Gulf of Mexico. Cold-water species may extend their ranges southward and shoreward during the winter. These movements may be rather general or distinctly migratory.

Pacific Coast

The Pacific Coast is dominated by a southward-flowing, cold, boundary current, the California Current. Sea temperatures vary little from north to south and, except for some protected bays in the south, are quite cold all the way to Baja California. Most Pacific fishes therefore have broad latitudinal distributions along that coast where some 709 species occur in

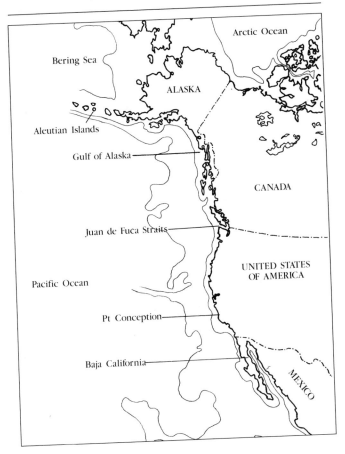

shelf waters (less than 660ft (200m)). Faunal boundaries are less well defined along the Pacific Coast than along the Atlantic Coast. Off Point Conception, California, the California Current moves offshore taking with it the fog bank. Many species, whose main distributions lie south of the USA, enter southern California but do not extend northward beyond this Point.

The Aleutian Islands mark the southern edge of Arctic conditions and the fish fauna of the Chuckchi and Bering Seas to the north is much less rich than that of the North Pacific Ocean and Gulf of Alaska to the south. Because of the steep profile of the Pacific Coast, very large seas may be generated and winter storms create extremely harsh coastal conditions which reshape and steepen the beaches. Small species may be sheltered by the rock structures, and kelp beds may dampen the seas, but many species retreat to deeper waters during these storms. The depths at which fishes can be caught from the shore are much greater for Pacific than for Atlantic species as a rule. Party boats operating from Atlantic ports fish in more shallow waters than those operating in the Juan de Fuca Straits or off Newport, Oregon.

The Descriptions

In selecting species for inclusion in this book I have been guided by two desires: to give sufficient representation so that the reader will appreciate the diversity of the marine fish fauna of North America and, at the same time, to be as inclusive as possible of the fishes most likely to be encountered when fishing, snorkeling, walking along the beach wrack or poking about in tidepools. Food and sport fishes, especially those caught from the shore or from party boats, and the pelagic big game species, are included. All-tackle world records, as listed by the International Game Fish Association (IGFA), are given for the larger species. Tropical fish families which occur only near the southernmost limit are mostly represented by a single species with some statement as to how many occur in North American waters. Because this is an introduction to the North American fish fauna and the species are representative to an extent, details of closely related species with differing features are omitted.

The Identification section pays special attention to distinctive features of body form, color, pattern, and structure that are easily seen and which may be checked against the illustration for more detail than is possible in the space of the written account. Thus, the description may call attention to a dark spot on the dorsal fin but the illustration will show how large it is and precisely where it occurs. Because a fish's geographical range and its ecological requirements are so closely related, these categories are combined into a single heading Range and Habitat. The Comments section notes the fishes' importance, interesting aspects of life-history, and a variety of other observations.

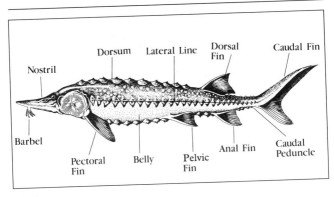

Glossary

Adipose Fin A small, fleshy, rayless fin located on the midline of the back between the dorsal and caudal fins in catfishes, salmonids, and some other primitive fishes.

Anadromous A fish that spawns and spends its early life in fresh water but moves into the ocean where it attains sexual maturity and spends most of its life span, as in the American shad or Atlantic sturgeon.

Anal Fin Median, ventral unpaired fin situated posterior to the anus.

Anterior Toward the head end of a structure or the body.

Anus The exterior opening of the digestive tract; the vent.

Axil The area of the body immediately adjacent to the innermost ray of the pectoral or pelvic fins.

Barbel A slender, elongate, flexible process located near the mouth, snout, and chin areas; tactile and gustatory in function.

Belly Ventral surface posterior to the base of the pelvic fins and anterior to the anal fin.

Branched Ray A soft ray which is forked or branched away from its base.

Breast Ventral surface below the pectoral fins and anterior to the belly.

Canine Teeth Sharp, conical teeth in the front part of the jaws; conspicuously larger than the rest of the teeth.

Caudal Fin The main propulsive fin, at the tail end of the body. A median fin which varies widely in shape.

Caudal Peduncle The narrow region of the body in front of the caudal fin from the posterior end of the base of the anal fin to the base of the caudal fin.

Cheek The area between the eye and the preopercle bone.

Ciguatoxic Used to describe fish whose flesh carries the toxin for ciguatera, a debilitating but usually non-fatal disease of humans (e.g. yellowfin grouper, great baracuda, greater amberjack).

Circumpolar Occurring around the poles; in this book around the Arctic Ocean.

Cirrus A fleshy tab or tuft most often above the eye or top of head.

Clasper A modified pelvic fin in sharks, rays, and chimaeras, used in sexual intercourse.

Ctenoid Scales Thin scales that bear a patch of tiny spine-like prickles (ctenii) on the exposed (posterior) surface.

Cycloid Scales More or less rounded scales that are flat and bear no ctenii on their posterior (exposed) field.

Dimorphism Two body forms in the same species, often referring to differences between male and female.

Distal Farthest from point of attachment (e.g. free edge of fins, farthest from their bases).

Dorsal Referring to the back; used as an abbreviation for dorsal fin.

Dorsum The upper part of the body; the back.

Emarginate Having a distal margin notched, indented, or slightly forked.

Falcate A fin is said to be falcate when its margin is deeply concave or sickle-shaped.

Filament A thread-like process usually associated with the fins.

Fin-Ray A bony or cartilaginous rod supporting the fin membrane. Soft rays usually are segmented (cross-striated), often branched and flexible near their tips, whereas spines are not segmented, never branched, and usually are stiff to their sharp distal tips.

Fusiform Tapering gradually at both ends; spindle-shaped.

Gill Filaments Respiratory structures projecting posteriorly from gill arches.

Gill Membranes Membranes that close the gill cavity ventrolaterally, supported by the branchiostegals.

Gonopodium Modified, rod-like anal fin of male *Gambusia* used in the transfer of sperm to genital pore of female.

Heterocercal A type of tail of fishes in which the vertebral column turns upward into the dorsal lobe.

Inferior Beneath, lower, or on the ventral side; e.g. inferior mouth.

Keel Scales or tissue forming a sharp edge or ridge.

Lateral Line System of sensory tubules communicating to the body surface by pores; refers most often to a longitudinal row of scales that bear tubules and visible pores; considered incomplete if only anterior scales possess pores and complete if all scales in that row (to base of caudal fin) have pores.

Lobes Elongate or extended parts of a fin, especially the upper and lower lobes of the caudal fin and the anterior lobe of the dorsal or anal fin.

Lunate Used to describe a deeply forked caudal fin as in the swordfish.

Median Said of a structure located along the longitudinal midline of the body.

Mesopelagic Occurring in the open ocean between 660–3300ft (200–1000m).

Nape Dorsal part of the body from the occiput to dorsal fin origin.

Non-protractile Not protrusible; premaxillaries are non-protractile if they are not fully separated from the snout continuous groove.

Occiput The posterior dorsal extremity of the head, often marked by the line separating scaly and scaleless portions of the dorsum.

Ocellus An eye-like spot, usually round with a light or dark border.

Opercle The large posterior bone of the gill cover; may be spiny, serrate, or entire (smooth).

Operculum Bony flap covering the gills of fishes, also called the gill cover.

Origin (or fins) Anterior end of the base of a dorsal fin or anal fin.

Ovate Outline egg-shaped.

Papillose Covered with small, nipple-like projections.

Pectoral Fin The anteriormost paired fin on the side, or on the breast, behind the head.

Pelagic Of open waters; usually referring to lakes.

Pelvic Fin The ventral-paired fin, lying below the pectoral fin or below the pectoral fin or between it and the anal fin.

Posteriad In a posterior direction.

Preopercle Sickle-shaped bone lying behind and below the eye; may be serrated or smooth.

Principal Rays Fin-rays that extend to the distal margin of caudal fins; enumerated by counting only one unbranched ray anteriorly above and below plus all branched rays between them.

Protrusible Used to describe the mouth when it is capable of being extended forward or downward from the head.

Proximal Nearer the body; center or base of attachment.

Saddle Rectangular or linear bars or bands which cross the back and extend partially or entirely downward across the sides.

Scute A modified scale in the form of a horny or bony plate which is often spiny or keeled.

Serrate Toothed or notched on the edge, like a saw.

Spiracle Opening on the back part of the head (above and behind the eye) in paddlefish and some sturgeons, representing a primitive gill cleft.

Striations Streaked or striped by narrow parallel lines or grooves.

Subopercle Bone immediately below the opercle in the operculum.

Supramaxilla Small, wedge-shaped movable bone adherent to the upper edge of the maxilla near its posterior tip.

Terminal Mouth When the upper and the lower jaws from the extreme anterior tip of the head.

Thoracic Pertaining to the chest region in fishes; pelvic fins thoracic when inserted below the pectoral fins.

Truncate Used to describe the body or a structure which is shortened and with a very steep profile.

Tubercle A small projection or lump; refers to keratinized or osseus structures developed during the breeding period.

Venter The belly or lower sides of a fish.

Ventral Pertaining to the lower surface.

Vermiculate Worm-like; marked with irregular or wavy lines.

Vestigial Used to describe a structure that is nearly absent or much reduced in size from normal and which may not be fully functional, at least in the original sense.

Vomer A median bone, usually bearing teeth, at the anterior extremity of the roof of the mouth.

Marine Fish Fauna

The species accounts which follow are arranged in a generally accepted phylogenetic sequence from primitive and archaic forms to the most highly derived forms. They are selected to be representative of the North American fish fauna with emphasis on food and game species, common species likely to be encountered in tide pools and shallow coastal waters, and species with peculiar habits or special structures.

Jawless Fishes

Pacific hagfish
Eptatretus stouti

25in (64cm)

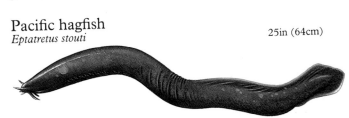

Identification Six barbels around mouth. Ten to 14 gill openings on each side of head. No paired fins. Eyes vestigial. Eel-like. Very slimy.
Range and Habitat Southern Alaska to Baja California on muddy bottom, mostly in deep water but occasionally to 30ft (9m).
Comments Three hagfishes (one Atlantic, two Pacific) occur in North America shallower than 660ft (200m). All attack dead, dying or trapped fish, eating the flesh and leaving a sack of bones and scales. Universally hated by commercial fishermen.

Sea lamprey
Petromyzon marinus

39in (1m)

Identification Seven gill openings behind large eye. No barbels. No paired fins. Mouth with disk and many rows of horny teeth. Eel-like.
Range and Habitat Temperate North America, from Gulf of St Lawrence to North Carolina (rarely northern Florida).
Comments Attacks living fishes by attaching to side and rasping a hole through which body fluids are sucked. Most lampreys are exclusively freshwater; those that enter the sea (one Atlantic, three Pacific) return to fresh water to spawn.

Cartilaginous Fishes

Spotted ratfish
Hydrolagus colliei

39in (1m)

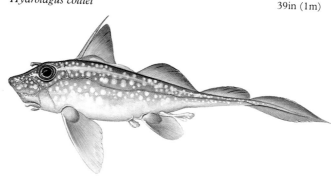

Identification Large head and long, tapering portion of body. Large spine at front of dorsal fin. Many white spots on darker iridescent body. Lateral line canals well developed. Eye large. Males with median clasper at head and at rear of each pelvic fin. Pectoral fins large.

Range and Habitat Southern Alaska to Baja California, mostly between 330-990ft (100-300m) from close to shore in north to 3000ft (914m) in south.

Comments Swims mostly with pectoral fins. Feeds mainly on shellfish and crustaceans. Other chimaeras occur in deep water along the east coast of North America.

Sixgill shark
Hexanchus griseus

16ft (4.8m)

Identification Single small dorsal fin above anus. Six gill slits. Body stout with broad head. Teeth in lower jaw comb-like.

Range and Habitat Nearly worldwide; from North Carolina to Florida and Gulf of Mexico and Aleutians to Baja California, and from surface to 6180ft (1883m), mostly deep water.

Comments Caught with a wide variety of commercial gear and used for food, in fish meal, and for oil.

Horn shark
Heterodontus francisci   4ft (1.2m)

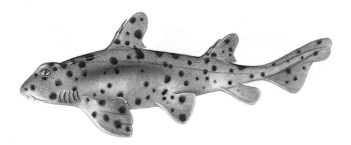

Identification Two large dorsal fins, each with strong spine at front.
Head large, blunt. Body has small, dark spots.
Range and Habitat California to New Mexico; also northwest South
America. Shallows to 500ft (150m).
Comments Two related species occur in east Pacific but south of
USA. All bullhead sharks lay large oval egg-cases with broad spiral
rim.

Nurse shark
Ginglymostoma cirratum   14ft (4.3m) usually less than 10ft (3m)

Identification Entirely brown, usually with yellow to russet tones.
Two dorsal fins nearly equal in size.
Range and Habitat South New England to southern Brazil.
Common in shallow coastal waters and large bays and around coral
reefs.
Comments Hide once much valued for leather. This sluggish species
is commonly encountered by divers who often treat it with disdain and
are bitten for their efforts. Usually it is inoffensive.

Whale shark
Rhincodon typus　　　　　40ft (12.1m) reputedly to 60ft (18.3m)

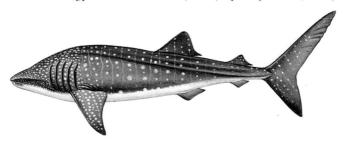

Identification Checkerboard pattern of whitish bars and stripes with
a large whitish spot in each square. Three long ridges along upper
side, mouth wide, nearly terminal.
Range and Habitat Worldwide in tropical and temperate seas; in
North America from New York and southern California southward.
Comments The largest of the sharks. Generally feeds on small
crustaceans and small fishes but will take larger prey caught on long
lines.

Sand tiger
Odontaspis taurus　　　　　　　　　　10½ft (3.2m)

Identification Two dorsal fins of nearly equal size, first closer to
pelvic than pectoral base. Teeth have long, narrow, central cusp and
two small lateral cusps. Often has dark spots.
Range and Habitat New Brunswick to Florida and northern Gulf of
Mexico; also known from east and southwest Atlantic, and Indo-west
Pacific oceans. From the surf zone to 660ft (200m).
Comments One young retained in each duct where it feeds on other
embryos and eggs. Birth is at an advanced state. A fish eater, of little
danger to man; attacks in Australia (where it is known as gray nurse
shark) apparently based on other sharks.

Thresher shark
Alopias vulpinus   18ft (5.5m) possibly 20ft (6.1m)

Identification Upper lobe of caudal fin almost as long as rest of
body. Snout conical.
Range and Habitat Worldwide in temperate and tropical seas, from
Gulf of St Lawrence and British Columbia southward.
Comments Caught commercially and sold fresh, dried or salted.
Hide used for leather. The bigeye thresher, *A.superciliosus*, with huge,
vertically elongate eye and a deep groove above eye, occurs off both
coasts. A third species occurs off northwestern Mexico.

Basking shark
Cetorhinus maximus   45ft (13.7m) but usually to 30ft (9.1m)

Identification Huge gill slits; keel in caudal peduncle; caudal fin
rather symmetrical, mouth large with very small teeth.
Range and Habitat Nearly worldwide in temperate waters, from
Newfoundland to Florida and Aleutians to Gulf of California.
Comments Feeds on plankton. Second largest of sharks.

Megamouth shark
Megachasma pelagios   15ft (4.5m)

Identification Large, terminal mouth with tiny teeth; rather small dorsal fin. Caudal fins with upper lobe much longer than lower and without a keel or peduncle. Blackish.
Range and Habitat California, Hawaii, Australia and Japan; probably widespread in Pacific seas.
Comments This recently discovered filter-feeding pelagic shark has excited much interest. Believed to be related to basking shark.

White shark
Carcharodon carcharias   20ft (6.1m)

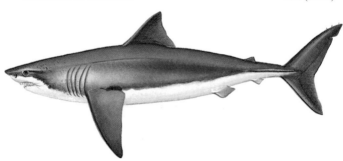

Identification Dark above, whitish below with pointed snout and large mouth with serrate triangular teeth. Dark smudge above axil of pectoral fin. Caudal nearly symmetrical with wide peduncular keel.
Range and Habitat Nearly worldwide in North America from Newfoundland and Gulf of Alaska southward. Oceanic but readily enters coastal waters, even into bays.
Comments A very dangerous and notorious shark. Young commonly feed on small ground sharks. Large adults known to gather around pods of whales off New England and off seal-pupping grounds in Pacific. Reports of white sharks larger than 20ft (6.1m) are erroneous.

Shortfin mako
Isurus oxyrinchus 13ft (4m)

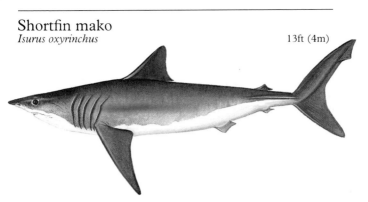

Identification Dark bluish above, white below. Snout pointed.
Caudal fin nearly symmetrical, lunate with peduncular keel. Teeth
long and narrow.
Range and Habitat Worldwide in tropical and temperate seas. From
southeastern Canada and Oregon southward. Mostly oceanic but has
been seen on reefs.
Comments A premier game fish known for its spectacular leaps.
Recent capture of 1207lbs (547.5kg) mako at Hawaii is largest by a
sport fisherman, but does not qualify under IGFA rules. A dangerous
shark. An important food fish.

Salmon shark
Lamna ditropis 10ft (3m)

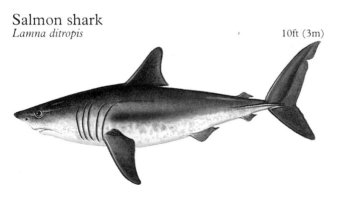

Identification Very deep, rounded body with large, nearly
symmetrical caudal fin and broad peduncular keel. Snout short.
Range and Habitat North Pacific; from Bering Sea to Baja
California.
Comments This shark is destructive to salmon and other
commercial fisheries and to fishing gear, particularly salmon nets. The
porbeagle, *Lamna nasus*, of the North Atlantic is closely related but
more slender and with a more pointed snout.

Tiger shark
Galeocerdo cuvier

24ft (7.3m)

Identification Snout short, broadly rounded from above. Body (except in very large adults) has dark blotches and bars above. Well-developed upper labial furrow.
Range and Habitat Worldwide mostly in tropical waters. From Cape Cod and southern California southward. Oceanic but enters bays and coastal waters, especially at night.
Comments A very dangerous, aggressive shark.

Smooth hammerhead
Sphyrna zygaena

13ft (4m)

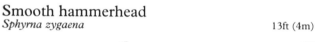

Identification Head laterally expanded, with eyes at lateral edge. Front edge of head rounded, first dorsal fin very large.
Range and Habitat Nearly worldwide in temperate waters; in North America from southeast Canada to Florida and California to northwest Mexico. Moves southward (e.g. to Florida) in winter.
Comments Seven of the nine species of hammerheads occur in the Americas, three reaching both coasts of the USA and an additional species reaching California. All differ in the shape of the head.

Greenland shark
Somniosus microcephalus   24ft (7.3m) usually 14ft (4.3m)

Identification Both dorsal fins small, without spines. No anal fin.
Spiracle present. Eye small. Snout short, rounded.
Range and Habitat North Atlantic ocean, from Baffin Bay and
northwestern Greenland to Maine; from estuaries and coastal bays to
3937ft (1200m) occurring deeper in south and in summer.
Comments Extensively used in Greenland for food and oil. Fresh
meat is toxic. Feeds on large fishes, seals and small whales. The
Pacific sleeper shark, *S. pacificus*, occurs from northern Alaska to Baja
California.

Spiny dogfish
Squalus acanthias   5ft (1.5m)

Identification Both dorsal fins have spine. The first much shorter
than fin. No anal fin. Gray with scattered white spots.
Range and Habitat Nearly worldwide in temperate waters in North
America from southern Greenland and Labrador to North Carolina
(rarely Florida) and Bering Sea to Baja California. From shore waters
(in north) to 600ft (183m).
Comments Commonly used as a laboratory animal in anatomy
classes. Heavily fished, more so in northeastern Atlantic. Commonly
sold in "fish and chips" emporia.

Pacific angel shark
Squatina californica

5ft (1.5m)

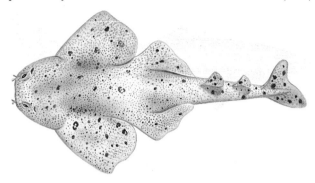

Identification Body flattened, deep division between head and pectoral fins. Gill openings lateral in that cleft.
Range and Habitat Southeastern Alaska to Gulf of California. Also from Ecuador to Chile, mainly in shallow, coastal waters but to 600ft (183m).
Comments The 12 angel sharks all look very much alike. *S. dumeril*, the Atlantic angel shark, occurs on the Atlantic coast from New England to Venezuela.

Largetooth sawfish
Pristis pristis

20ft (6.1m)

Identification Gill openings in ventral side of head. Snout forms a large sword with 20 or fewer teeth on each side. First dorsal fin origin is in front of pelvic fin origin.
Range and Habitat Florida and north Gulf of Mexico to Brazil, in shallow coastal and estuarine waters. Enters fresh water in tropics.
Comments Formerly harpooned but now regarded as a curiosity of nature to be protected. Does not pose a danger unless speared or hooked.

Pacific electric ray
Torpedo californica   4½ft (1.4m)

Identification Disk rounded, two dorsals and large caudal fin.
Range and Habitat British Columbia to Baja California from shore to 900ft (274m).
Comments Capable of producing electric shock but of no danger unless handled. Similar to the Atlantic torpedo, *T. mobiliana*, which ranges from Nova Scotia to Carolinas and, in winter, to Florida.

Atlantic guitarfish
Rhinobatos lentiginosus

30in (76cm)

Identification Body flattened. Pectoral fins fused to head to form triangular outline from above. Two dorsal fins well developed.
Range and Habitat North Carolina to eastern Mexico, moving south and shoreward in winter.
Comments Related species occur in east Pacific from California southward and in the Caribbean.

Clearnose skate
Raja eglanteria

33in (84cm)

Identification Broad transparent area on each side of snout tip. Dorsal side of disk has dark markings.
Range and Habitat Massachusetts to Gulf of Mexico; abundant inshore especially during warm months.
Comments Commonly caught by anglers fishing from piers and jetties.

Barndoor skate
Raja laevis   5ft (1.5m)

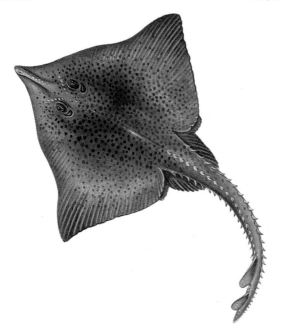

Identification Snout very pointed, disk broad, angular. Underside of disk has blackish pores.
Range and Habitat Southeastern Canada to North Carolina from shore to deep water, occurring to water's edge in north.
Comments Not utilized at present except for processing into fish meal. Commonly caught by anglers.

Winter skate
Raja ocellata

43in (1.1m)

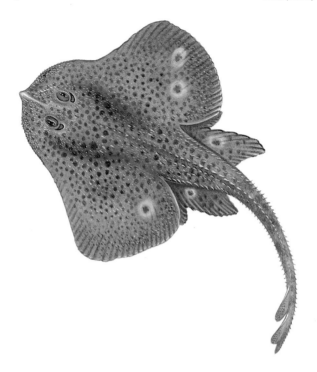

Identification Tail rather broad with many rows of stout spines above extending forward to back. Usually has ocellated spots on upper side of disk. Disk rounded.

Range and Habitat Gulf of St Lawrence and Newfoundland to Cape Hatteras, from the shore to 1225ft (373m); most common inshore in the winter.

Comments In addition to the five skates included here, 16 other skates (eight Atlantic, eight Pacific) of the very similar genera, *Raja* and *Breviraja*, occur in coastal and shelf waters of North America. They differ mainly in the shape and proportions of the disk, the nature and extent of spination, and in details of pigmentation. They are part of the by-catch of other fisheries and are used in fish meal.

Longnose skate
Raja rhina

4½ft (1.4m)

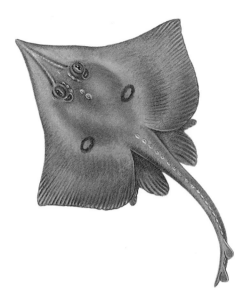

Identification Snout, long and pointed, front edge of disk concave. Brown above with darker ring at base of each pectoral fin. One row of spines on top of tail.
Range and Habitat South Alaska to Baja California in water shelf and slope waters to depths of 2000ft (610m).
Comments ›Fished commercially in some areas.

Starry skate
Raja stellulata

30in (76cm)

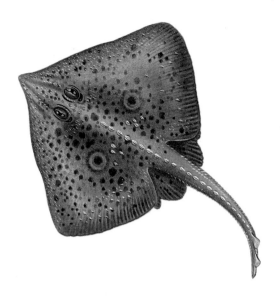

Identification Row of very strong spines along midline of back and tail. Ocellus often present near base of each pectoral fin. Snout short, disk rounded laterally.
Range and Habitat Bering Sea to Baja California from 60ft (18.3m) to more than 2000ft (610m).
Comments Common around islands of British Columbia.

Pelagic stingray
Dasyatis violacea

64in (1.6m)

Identification Dark brownish violet, disk broadly rounded in front.
Long spine toward base of tail.
Range and Habitat Worldwide pelagic ray occurring in North
America from southeastern Canada to Middle Atlantic states and
British Columbia to Baja California.
Comments In addition to this pelagic species, four other Atlantic
and one Pacific species occur in coastal waters and bays. Their spines
can inflict a nasty wound if the ray is handled or stepped on.

Yellow stingray
Urolophus jamaicensis   26in (66cm)

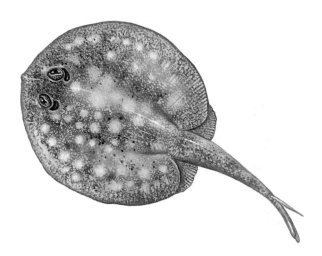

Identification Disk round, yellowish with dark markings. Tail has spine.

Range and Habitat North Carolina to South America from shore to 600ft (183m); common near grass beds and reefs in shallow coastal water.

Comments Commonly seen by divers and snorkelers. The related round stingray, *U. halleri*, occurs along the Pacific coast from California to Panama.

Bat ray
Myliobatis californicus

6ft (1.8m) across disk

Identification Disk very broad, pointed, wing-like. Head deep, blunt. Tail long, whip-like with spine at base behind small dorsal fin.
Range and Habitat Oregon to New Mexico.
Comments Swims by "flapping" its wings. Eats shellfish and crustaceans. Additional related species occur on both coasts of North America. They sometimes gather in very large schools (to 1500) in the non-breeding season.

Manta
Manta birostris

22ft (6.7m) across wings

Identification Head large with two large forward-projecting flaps, mouth terminal. Blackish above, white below; usually has large white areas on back.

Range and Habitat Nearly worldwide, most common in warm waters; in North America from southeast Canada and Bermuda and southern California southward. Pelagic.

Comments Largest of the rays, commonly found well out to sea but entering coastal areas where the water is clear. Northern records occur during the summer and often in association with Gulf Stream eddies and rings.

Bony Fishes

Green sturgeon
Acipenser medirostris   7ft (2.1m)

Identification Five rows of scutes on body, one to two scutes behind dorsal fin. Weighs up to 300lbs (136kg).
Range and Habitat North Pacific, from Alaska to Baja California.
Comments One of two sturgeons in North American Pacific; the other, white sturgeon, *A. transmontanus*, is less massive and lacks the scutes behind dorsal fin. It also is much larger, 20ft (6.1m) and possibly 1800lbs (816kg).

Atlantic sturgeon
Acipenser oxyrhynchus   15ft (4.5m)

Identification Five rows of scutes on body. Snout long, pointed. Weighs up to 800lbs (363kg)
Range and Habitat Labrador to Florida and east Gulf of Mexico. Anadromous.
Comments Commercially important for meat and caviar but the stocks are severely depleted and catches are low. In most states and provinces it is listed as threatened or of special concern. The smaller shortnose sturgeon (*A. brevirostris*) of the Atlantic coast is more estuarine and much smaller. It has a blunter snout.

Tarpon
Megalops atlanticus

8ft (2.4m)

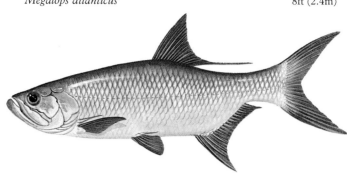

Identification Dorsal fin has last ray filamentous. Very large silvery scales. Back dark, mouth oblique, large. Weighs up to 300lbs (136kg)
Range and Habitat Southeastern Canada and Bermuda to Brazil. Also in Gulf of Guinea.
Comments Juveniles common in fresh water. A very important game fish noted for its spectacular leaps. World record 283lbs (128kg).

Bonefish
Albula vulpes

41in (1m)

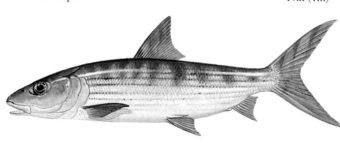

Identification Long, conical snout, its tip blackish, mouth inferior. Streamlined body, silvery with dark back.
Range and Habitat Southeastern Canada to Brazil; possibly nearly worldwide in tropics but status of various populations unclear.
Comments A premier game fish. World record 19lbs (8.6kg), usually fished from small boat in shallow flats and with light tackle. Good to eat but very bony.

American eel
Anguilla rostrata 5ft (1.5m)

Identification Body with elongate, embedded scales, arranged in basket-weaver fashion. Dorsal fins begin farther forward than anal fin.
Range and Habitat Southwestern Greenland and Labrador to South America.
Comments Probably not specifically distinct from the European eel, *A. anguilla*. Adults live in fresh water and navigate to the sea to spawn and die. Larvae spend about one year at sea, metamorphose into elvers and enter the estuaries. Commercially important. Females decidedly larger than males.

Green moray
Gymnothorax funebris 8ft (2.4m)

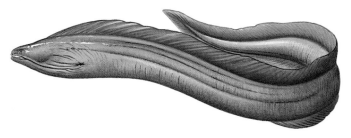

Identification Entirely dark green to bright green. No pectoral fins. Dorsal fin starts on top of head. Body thick.
Range and Habitat Bermuda and North Carolina to Brazil but adults have been captured as far north as Nova Scotia.
Comments Seventeen other morays occur in Atlantic waters of North America (mostly in the southeastern USA) and one is in the Pacific. The green moray and the stout moray, *Muraena robusta*, are by far the largest. Morays have strong jaws and sharp teeth and can be dangerous if attacked. Left alone, they generally do not bother divers. The jaw gaping is part of a pumping action that moves water over the gills and is not a threat.

Snubnose eel
Simenchelys parasitica   24in (61cm)

Identification Snout short, mouth terminal, a horizontal slit. Body
has elongated scales arranged in basket-weave fashion. Dorsal fin
begins above and slightly behind tip of pectoral fin.
Range and Habitat Banks off Newfoundland to Florida and in
Bahamas but also in eastern Atlantic and western and south Pacific;
always in cold water.
Comments Feeds on flesh of larger fishes (possibly dead, dying, or
trapped) much like hagfishes and, like hagfishes, they produce much
slime. Caught fairly commonly on the banks off southeast Canada and
New England.

Hardhead catfish
Arius felis   24in (61cm)

Identification Body without scales. Long, strong, serrated spine at
front of dorsal and pectoral fins, these provided with locking
mechanisms. Four barbels in chin and one at each corner of mouth.
Range and Habitat Massachusetts to Mexico and possibly farther
south, in shallow coastal waters, especially in bays and estuaries.
Absent from clear waters and offshore islands.
Comments Although commonly caught by bridge and surf
fishermen, this catfish is usually discarded although it is edible. Two
other marine catfishes (*Bagre*) occur, one on each coast.

Blueback herring
Alosa aestivalis

15in (38cm)

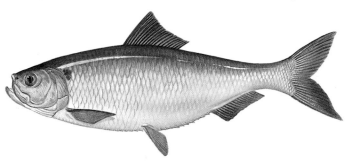

Identification Scuted belly, silvery on sides, dark above.
Range and Habitat Nova Scotia to Florida in coastal waters,
running upstream to spawn.
Comments Harvested with other river herrings and usually marketed
with the alewife, *A. pseudoharengus*. These two run the rivers along
with the hickory shad, *A. mediocris*, and the American shad, *A.
sapidissima* .

American shad
Alosa sapidissima

30in (76cm)

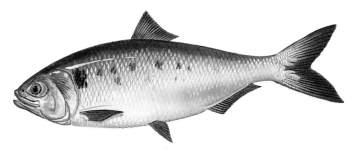

Identification Belly scuted, silvery with darker back. Large spot at
shoulder with other spots along upper side.
Range and Habitat Labrador to northeastern Florida in coastal
waters, bays and estuaries running up rivers to spawn. Introduced into
Pacific waters where it now occurs from Alaska to Baja California.
Comments Historically, one of the very important food fishes of the
New World. Still popular as a food and sport fish but landings much
reduced over earlier periods. Very similar to the Alabama shad
(*A. alabame*) which replaces it in the northern Gulf of Mexico.

Atlantic menhaden
Brevoortia tyrannus   18½in (47cm)

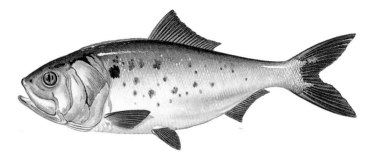

Identification Fatty ridge on midback in front of dorsal fin. Scales
with rear edge comb-like. Dark shoulder spot with many smaller dark
spots on sides.
Range and Habitat Gulf of St Lawrence to Florida in coastal
waters. Not anadromous.
Comments Three other very similar species of *Brevoortia* occur in
large schools only in eastern North America, two of them in the
northern Gulf of Mexico, the other along the southeastern USA and
Gulf of Mexico. They differ in scale size and fin color. All are
important commercially for fish meal and oil.

Pacific herring
Clupea pallasi   18in (46cm)

Identification Belly weakly scuted. Silvery with darker back and no
spots.
Range and Habitat North Pacific, from Arctic-Alaska to Baja
California.
Comments This, and the very similar Atlantic herring, *C. harengus*,
which occurs from western Greenland and Labrador to North
Carolina, are prized food fishes, both for the flesh and roe, and as a
source of fish oil. Stocks in both oceans are now reduced.

Round herring
Etrumeus teres   12in (30cm)

Identification Belly without scutes, elongate and rounded in cross-section; silvery with dark back.
Range and Habitat Nova Scotia to northern Florida and in Gulf of Mexico; on Pacific Coast from California to Chile.
Comments Fished commercially in the Gulf of Maine. The Pacific populations are sometimes regarded as a separate species.

Striped anchovy
Anchoa hepsetus   6in (15cm)

Identification Mouth inferior, upper jaw extending well behind eye. Snout short. Narrow silver stripe on side.
Range and Habitat Nova Scotia to Florida and Gulf of Mexico; rare north of New Jersey in shallow coastal waters including bays and inlets.
Comments Representative of 13 species of anchovies which occur in coastal waters of North America. All are very similar. Although abundant, they are harvested only locally, usually to be served deep-fried in restaurants with a Latin cuisine. The canned anchovy market is supplied largely from southern Europe because of lower production costs.

Capelin
Mallotus villosus

10in (25cm)

Identification Adipose fin large, rectangular; lower jaw projecting.
Scales very small. Males have large, rounded, paired fins and two
bands of modified scales alongside.
Range and Habitat Circumpolar, south to Cape Cod and Straits of
Juan de Fuca.
Comments An extremely important forage fish, occurring in
immense schools. Although dried and used for food in some areas,
most is processed for fish meal and oil. It is also used for bait and as
fertilizer. Stocks have declined.

Rainbow smelt
Osmerus mordax

14in (36cm)

Identification Adipose fin small; lower jaw not longer than upper.
Scales larger than capelin.
Range and Habitat Labrador to New Jersey and western Arctic to
British Columbia, running up rivers to spawn.
Comments An important commercial and recreational fish, fished
more with small seines and dip-nets during the spawning run than
with hook and line. Usually prepared deep-fried, whole.

Eulachon
Thalichthys pacificus   9in (23cm)

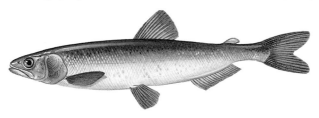

Identification Gill cover has concentric striations. Anal fin low with long base.
Range and Habitat Bering Sea to coastal California; anadromous.
Comments Important to Indians for food and oil. Its oil is solid at room temperature. Sometimes threaded with a wick and used as a candle, hence its common name, candlefish. Its exploitation in part of its range is reserved for Indians. Five other smelts occur along the Pacific coast.

Atlantic whitefish
Coregonus huntsmani   20in (51cm)

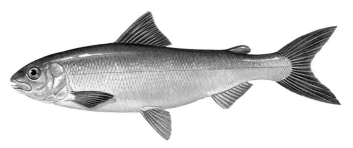

Identification Mostly silvery, bluish above. Jaws about equal, mouth nearly terminal.
Range and Habitat Nova Scotia, anadromous.
Comments Commonly confused with lake whitefish, *C. clupeaformis*, which rarely occurs in salt water. Food fish, but rather rare; regarded as endangered.

Pink salmon
Oncorhynchus gorbuscha   30in (76cm)

Identification Silvery with dark spots on upper sides and caudal fin. During spawning run, males have hooked jaws and strongly humped backs in front of dorsal fin, and sides rosy. Scales small, more than 150 in lateral line.
Range and Habitat Arctic Ocean to California, also in northwestern Pacific. Anadromous. Introduced many times into Atlantic waters but not established except in upper Great Lakes.
Comments A valuable food and sport fish; world record 12lb 9oz (5.7kg).

Chum salmon
Oncorhynchus keta   40in (1m)

Identification Body and fins unspotted. Silvery, with darker back. During spawning run, males have jaws only slightly hooked, white tip on anal and pelvic fins, and dark reddish bars along lower side.
Range and Habitat Arctic-Alaska to California, also in northwestern Pacific. Anadromous.
Comments A valuable food and sport fish, world record 37lbs (16.8kg). Flesh not so highly regarded as other salmons, but is excellent smoked.

Coho salmon
Oncorhynchus kisutch

38in (96cm)

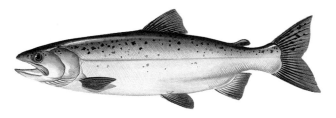

Identification Dark spots on upper back and upper lobe (only) of caudal fin. Silvery, with darker back. During spawning run, males have hooked jaws and broad red stripe on side and often a dark belly.
Range and Habitat Gulf of Alaska to California. Anadromous. Introduced into New England waters and well established in Great Lakes.
Comments A valuable food and sport fish, world record 33lb 4oz (15.1kg). Also called silver salmon.

Sockeye salmon
Oncorhynchus nerka

33in (84cm)

Identification Silvery with no dark spots. On spawning run, males have strongly hooked jaws, white lower jaw, dark head and bright red body.
Range and Habitat Bering Sea to Columbia River. Anadromous.
Comments A valuable food and sport fish. World record 15lb 3oz (6.9kg). Most valuable fishery on Pacific coast of Canada. Also known as red sockeye salmon.

Rainbow trout
Oncorhynchus mykiss

45in (1.1m)

Identification Silvery with small black spots along upper parts, dorsal and caudal fins, and usually rimming the adipose fin. Broad, pale red stripe along side in fish ready to spawn and in landlocked populations.

Range and Habitat Native from Alaska to northern Baja California and in the northwest Pacific. Anadromous. Also extensive inland distribution west of the Divide in North America. Widely introduced, occurring along east coast of Newfoundland to Nova Scotia.

Comments Used extensively in aquaculture. An important food and sport fish, world record 42lb 2oz (19.1kg). Sea run fish are called steelheads.

Chinook salmon
Oncorhynchus tshawytscha

58in (1.5m)

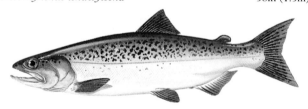

Identification Silvery with dark spots on upper body and caudal fin. On spawning run, males have moderately hooked jaws and red blotches along side.

Range and Habitat Bering Sea to California. Anadromous.

Comments A premier food and game fish; official world record 97lb 4oz (44kg) but fish at 135lbs (61.2kg) have been reported. The most highly prized of the Pacific salmon. Also called king salmon.

Arctic char
Salvelinus alpinus 38in (96cm)

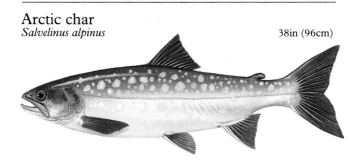

Identification Body dark with many large red and pallid spots on sides. Season fish usually silvery. Fins unspotted.
Range and Habitat Circumpolar, south on Atlantic coast to Newfoundland. Anadromous. Landlocked populations occur in New England lakes.
Comments Food and sport fish with historic importance to native peoples of North America. World record 32lb 9oz (14.8kg).

Dolly Varden
Salvelinus malma 36in (91cm)

Identification Dark bluish above with many large spots (red, cream-colored, yellowish). Very silvery in the sea.
Range and Habitat Bering Sea to Oregon, also in northwestern Pacific. Anadromous.
Comments Not highly regarded as a game fish. World record 12lbs (5.4kg).

Bull trout
Salvelinus confluentus

39in (1m)

Identification Dark with red, yellowish and cream-colored spots.
Range and Habitat Alaska to California mainly in fresh water but
caught in Pacific waters of Washington and British Columbia.
Comments Very similar to Dolly Varden but head larger, flatter
above. World record 32lbs (14.5kg), but known to reach 40lbs (18kg).

Brook trout
Salvelinus fontinalis

18in (46cm)

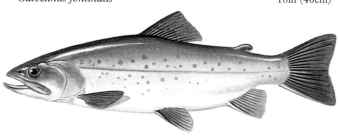

Identification Head and body dark, bluish to greenish above, white
below, with pale worm-like markings or marbling.
Range and Habitat Hudson Bay to New England. Anadromous.
Also extensive distribution in fresh water.
Comments World record 14lb 8oz (6.6kg). A favorite of the fly
fishermen.

Atlantic salmon
Salmo salar   5ft (1.5m)

Identification Silvery with blackish spots or X-markings. Caudal fin usually without spots.
Range and Habitat North Atlantic, from Labrador to Gulf of Maine. Widely introduced.
Comments A superb food and game fish, widely cultured in pens in coastal fjords and inlets. World record 79lb 12oz (36.2kg) but fish as large as 84lbs (38kg) are recorded.

Atlantic argentine
Argentina silus   24in (61cm)

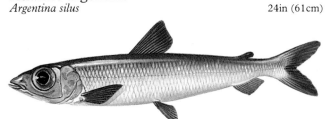

Identification Very large eye, small adipose fin. Silvery, sometimes brassy, on sides with darker back.
Range and Habitat North Atlantic, from Labrador to about Cape Cod.
Comments A minor food fish; the commercial catch along North American coasts is by foreign vessels and not landed locally. Two other very similar species occur in North America, one on each coast.

Snakefish
Trachinocephalus myops   15in (38cm)

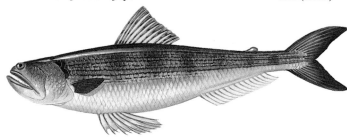

Identification Sandy-colored with blue and yellow stripes. Mouth oblique, head short and deep, snout blunt.
Range and Habitat Worldwide in warm temperate and tropical coastal waters. Along American coast from Nova Scotia to Brazil. Prefers open sandy areas around grass flats or reefs.
Comments Occasionally caught by anglers.

California lizardfish
Synodus lucioceps   20in (51cm)

Identification Head small, snout pointed. Mostly tan.
Range and Habitat California to New Mexico.
Comments Seven species of *Synodus* occur in Atlantic coastal waters of North America. They differ primarily in color, pattern and scale size.

Shortnose greeneye
Chloropthalmus agassizi   6in (15cm)

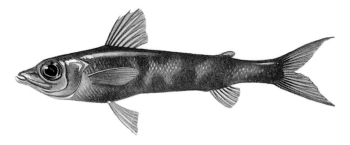

Identification Eye very large, green. Silvery with dark saddle. Mouth oblique, superior.
Range and Habitat Banks off Nova Scotia to South America in deep shelf and upper slope waters.
Comments Representative of a group of deep-dwelling lizardfishes that are common in waters along the edge of the shelf. All are hermaphroditic.

Longnose lancetfish
Alepisaurus ferox   7ft (2.1m)

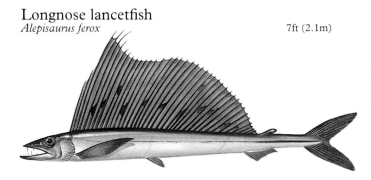

Identification Large sail-like dorsal fin, with first rays largest. Small adipose fin. Body soft, very flabby, silvery. Keel at tail. Teeth large, fang-like, hollow.
Range and Habitat Very wide-ranging; in North America from Nova Scotia to South America, and Alaska to Chile. Mesopelagic.
Comments Taken on long lines. A curiosity whose capture always evokes interest. Hermaphroditic. A closely related species, the shortnose lancetfish, *A. brevirostris*, has a rounded first dorsal fin.

Haddock
Melanogrammus aeglifinus   44in (1.1m)

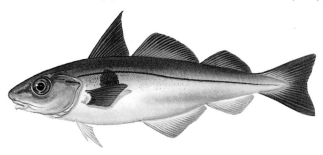

Identification Dark above, silvery to white on sides and belly. Large black blotch on side above pectoral fin. Lateral line black.
Range and Habitat Newfoundland to Cape Hatteras in coastal waters, deeper in winter. Also in eastern Atlantic.
Comments A prized food fish marketed fresh, frozen, canned or smoked (as Finnan Haddie). Overfished, stocks are down. World record 9lb 15oz (4.5kg).

Atlantic cod
Gadus morhua   6ft (1.8m)

Identification Three dorsal and two anal fins. Lateral line whitish. Sides with many brownish to reddish spots.
Range and Habitat North Atlantic, from southern Baffin Island to North Carolina in coastal waters.
Comments A food fish of tremendous historical and present-day importance and a sport fish. It is the subject of a multinational fishery, but caught by Canadian fishermen in North America waters. Also important industrially (isinglass, fish meal, oil, glue).

Pacific cod
Gadus macrocephalus   45in (1.1m)

Identification Pacific representative of Atlantic cod. Pale blotches along side.
Range and Habitat North Pacific, along North America coast from Bering Sea to California.
Comments Very important commercially in British Columbia.

Walleye pollack
Theragra chalcogramma   36in (91cm)

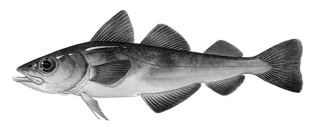

Identification Three dorsal fins, second dorsal begins above first dorsal fin; two anal fins. Chin barbel very small. Dark with pale mottling. Body elongate.
Range and Habitat North Pacific, from Bering Sea to California, usually in deeper shelf waters.
Comments Formerly used primarily for animal food (mink) but now a major commercial resource used in production of surimi.

Red hake
Urophycis chuss

20in (51cm)

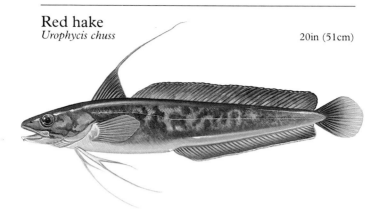

Identification Reddish, mottled dark. Pelvic fins reach just beyond origin of anal fin. Two dorsal fins, first with three long filaments.
Range and Habitat Labrador to North Carolina from near shore in north to deep water 3000ft (914m) in south.
Comments An important food fish.

White hake
Urophycis tenuis

53in (1.3m)

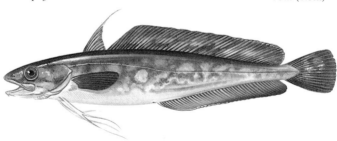

Identification Pelvic fins reach about to anus. Filament on dorsal fin short.
Range and Habitat Labrador to North Carolina (rarely to Florida), in deep shelf and upper slope waters (660–3380ft (200–1030m)).
Comments A large fish, reaching 50lbs (22.7kg), commercially valuable and landed in great quantities, usually in combination with red hake. Also caught by sport fishermen, world record 46lb 4oz (21kg).

Longfin hake
Urophycis chesteri

15in (38cm)

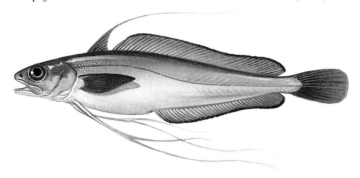

Identification Pelvic fins reach about to caudal peduncle, dorsal filament long. Dorsal and anal fins with dark margin.
Range and Habitat Labrador to Florida in deep shelf and upper slope waters (600–1290ft (183–393m)).
Comments Soft flesh, less important than red or white hake, mostly processed into meal and oil. Four additional species of the genus *Urophycis* also occur along the Atlantic coast of North America.

Pacific hake
Merluccius productus

36in (91cm)

Identification Second dorsal and anal fin with a deep indentation but not divided into two fins. Teeth prominent, sharp. Mouth large. Silvery, with dark back and often with metallic reflection.
Range and Habitat Alaska to Gulf of California (also northwestern Pacific) in deep shelf or slope waters.
Comments Two very similar species occur along Atlantic coast of North America. All are commercially important, with much of the catch taken by foreign vessels.

Cusk
Brosme brosme

40in (1m)

Identification One long dorsal and anal fin. Caudal rounded. Pelvic fins short. Body stout. Usually dark reddish brown.
Range and Habitat Southern Labrador to New Jersey (also in eastern Atlantic) usually on rough bottoms.
Comments A commercial and sport species, usually taken with long lines. World record 32lb 13oz (14.9kg).

Marlin-spike
Nezumia bairdi

16in (40cm)

Identification Body tapering to long point without caudal fin. Anal fin higher than second dorsal fin. Triangular snout. Serrated spine in first dorsal fin.
Range and Habitat Gulf of St Lawrence to West Indies, occurring in shelf water in the north.
Comments Grenadiers are common in deeper slope waters. Only four other Atlantic and two Pacific species occur in North America in shelf water. Some are commercially important.

Spotted cusk-eel
Chilara taylori   14in (36cm)

Identification Dorsal, caudal, and anal fin. Scales on body elongate, arranged in basket-weave fashion. Pelvic fins with two rays, on throat below eye. Boldly spotted.
Range and Habitat Oregon to Baja California on sand bottom.
Comments Produces sound with swimbladder. Commonly caught by marine mammals and cormorants. Other very similar genera and species occur in North America, 14 along the Atlantic coast.

Fawn cusk-eel
Lepophidium profundorum   10in (25cm)

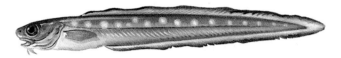

Identification Scales on head and body in regular rows. Dorsal, caudal and anal fins confluent, the tail pointed. Body brown with row of large pale spots.
Range and Habitat Southeast Canada to eastern Gulf of Mexico occurring in shallow water only in north.
Comments Related species, most of them in deeper water, occur only along the Atlantic coast.

Pearlfish
Carapus bermudensis

8½in (22cm)

Identification Scaleless, translucent, with long anal fin, the anus near the throat.

Range and Habitat Bermuda and south Florida to South America, from shallow tidal flats into slope waters.

Comments Lives in association with certain sea cucumbers (*Holo phuria*), entering their body cavity during the day, and emerging to forage openly at night.

Oyster toadfish
Opsanus tau

15in (38cm)

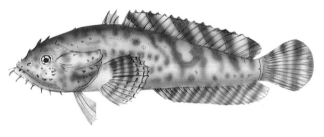

Identification Body stout, scaleless, with dark brown blotches. Fins with pale bars.

Range and Habitat Massachusetts Bay to Florida, in shallow coastal waters. Often lives in discarded tires and oil drums as well as rock jetties.

Comments Of some importance as a research animal because of its size and hardiness. A sound producer, especially during breeding season. A bait stealer, disliked by fishermen. Related species occur along the southern coast of USA.

Plainfish midshipman
Porichthys notatus   15in (38cm)

Identification Silvery with darker back, rows of photopores on sides and belly. Fins unmarked. Pelvic fins under head.
Range and Habitat Alaska to New Mexico from very shallow bays to slope water.
Comments This and related specklefin midshipman, *P. myriaster*, are noted as "singing" fish because of the loud sounds they produce. A related species occurs along the southeastern USA.

Goosefish
Lophius americanus   4ft (1.2m)

Identification Large depressed head with huge superior mouth and rows of long, sharp teeth. Gill openings behind stalked pectoral fin. Modified dorsal spines on head.
Range and Habitat Gulf of St Lawrence to Florida, from shore to slope waters. Common in bays and harbors in north.
Comments Tail part of body marketed as monkfish. Also used for fish meal. Fishermen generally regard it as a nuisance but world record is 37lb 7oz (17kg) and 50lbs (27kg) fish are known. Related genera and species occur off the southeastern or Gulf coast of USA.

Sargassumfish
Histrio histrio

8in (20cm)

Identification Body smooth, without prickles but with many fleshy tabs; yellowish with broad, dark brown markings. Stalked pectoral fin works like a "hand."

Range and Habitat Essentially worldwide, pelagic in sargassum community. In North America, from southeast Canada southward.

Comments Blown into shore during storms. The largest specimens are from Bermuda and northern locations. Many related species of frogfishes, *Antennarius*, occur along our coast. All species have a sandpapery body.

Atlantic batfish
Dibranchus atlanticus   16in (40cm) but usually much smaller

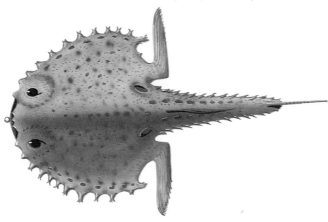

Identification Body flattened, spiny, anterior edge semicircular. Gill opening behind pectoral fins. Dark brown or blackish.
Range and Habitat An abundant species in slope waters from Gulf of St Lawrence to South America, also in eastern Atlantic, occasionally entering shelf waters in southeastern Canada.
Comments Representative of the Family Ogrocephalidae, of which ten other species occur in North American coastal waters.

Northern clingfish
Gobiesox meandricus 6½in (16cm)

Identification Large flattened head and body with suction disk on chest. No fin spines. Dorsal fin above anal fin.
Range and Habitat Southeastern Alaska to Baja California, mostly in rocky tidepools.
Comments Largest of two species on North American Pacific coast. Three additional species occur on Atlantic coast.

Spotfin flyingfish
Cypselurus furcatus 14in (36cm)

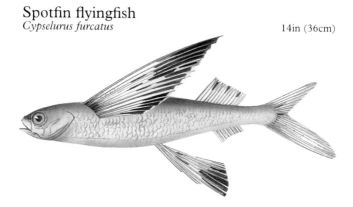

Identification Pectoral and pelvic fins very long, wing-like. Pectoral blackish with broad clear band. Pelvic fin has black tip.
Range and Habitat Nova Scotia to southern South America, pelagic but entering shore waters after storm; juvenile common in sargassum.
Comments Representative of 15 species of flyingfish that reach North American shores. Larger species are fished commercially around some tropical islands (e.g. Barbados).

Ballyhoo
Hemiramphus brasiliensis   16in (40cm)

Identification Lower jaw much longer than upper, orange-tipped. Pectoral fins short. Sides flattened, silvery. Lower lobe of caudal fin longest.
Range and Habitat Nova Scotia to Brazil, pelagic in shore waters.
Comments An important forage and bait fish. Seven other halfbeaks occur in North American coastal waters.

Flat needlefish
Ablennes hians   43in (1.1m)

Identification Both jaws very long with small sharp teeth, sides very flat, silvery with dark bars. Dorsal and anal fins far back, their margins falcate.
Range and Habitat Nearly worldwide in tropics, on Atlantic coast from Chesapeake Bay southward. Pelagic, oceanic but occasionally inshore along open coasts with clear water.
Comments Occasionally caught by anglers; world record 4lb 4oz (1.9kg).

Atlantic needlefish
Strongylura marina   24in (61cm)

Identification Both jaws very long. Body tubular, silvery with greenish back. Caudal fin bluish.
Range and Habitat Gulf of Maine to Brazil in coastal waters including bays, inlets and intracoastal waterways.
Comments Six other needlefish enter region. All feed on small fish.

Pacific saury
Cololabis saira

14in (36cm)

Identification Dorsal fin starts behind origin of anal fin. Five to seven finlets behind dorsal and anal fin. Snout pointed but without a long beak.
Range and Habitat Gulf of Alaska to Mexico, also in northwestern Pacific. Pelagic.
Comments An important forage fish for striped marlin, tunas. Fished commercially off Japan. Occurs in large schools.

Atlantic saury
Scomberesox saurus

20in (51cm)

Identification Similar to Pacific saury but jaws longer, forming a beak. Green spot above pectoral fin.
Range and Habitat Newfoundland to North Carolina, also in eastern Atlantic. Pelagic.
Comments Although occurring at times in large numbers, the resource is too variable for commercial exploitation. An important forage fish for pelagic predators.

Mummichog
Fundulus heteroclitus 5in (13cm)

Identification Sides mottled or spotted, with alternately dark and pale bars. Head black, snout rounded.
Range and Habitat Gulf of St Lawrence to Florida in estuaries, tidal creeks, and marshes.
Comments An important laboratory fish.

Striped killifish
Fundulus majalis 7in (18cm)

Identification Silvery with bold black stripes (Atlantic males) or bars (females, Gulf males).
Range and Habitat Gulf of Maine to northeastern Florida and northern Gulf of Mexico.
Comments Seven additional species of *Fundulus* occur along the Atlantic coast and one along the Pacific coast. All are littoral species in sheltered waters.

Eastern mosquitofish
Gambusia holbrooki 1½in (3.8cm); males smaller

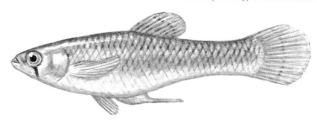

Identification Dark triangular bar under eye. Dark outline to scales create a diamond pattern. Males with anal fin forming a copulatory organ.
Range and Habitat New Jersey to northeastern Gulf of Mexico in littoral waters of tidal creeks and estuaries. Also extensive inland distribution.
Comments Introduced widely for mosquito control. Used in the laboratory. Its aggressiveness limits its use in the aquarium trade.

Topsmelt
Atherinops affinis 14½in (37cm)

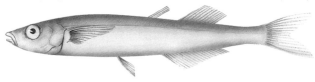

Identification Small first dorsal fin above anus. Broad silver stripe along side.
Range and Habitat British Columbia to northwestern Mexico in inshore waters, bays.
Comments A schooling species of commercial and limited angling importance.

Jacksmelt
Atherinopsis californiensis   17½in (44.5cm)

Identification Like topsmelt but with first dorsal fin distinctly in advance of anal fin.
Range and Habitat Oregon to Baja California in shallow coastal waters.
Comments Important food fish, also caught by anglers.

California grunion
Leuresthes tenuis   7½in (19cm)

Identification Like topsmelt but more slender and with first dorsal fin behind origin of anal fin.
Range and Habitat California and Baja California along beaches.
Comments Famous for habit of spawning on the beach at high-tide after the full and new moon. The eggs hatch during the next period of spring tides. Catching grunion on the beach at spawning time is a unique Californian "sport."

Atlantic silverside
Menidia menidia

6in (15cm)

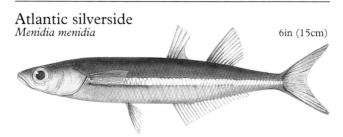

Identification Silvery stripe on side. Two separate dorsal fins. Edge of anal fin straight.
Range and Habitat Gulf of St Lawrence to Florida along sandy beaches and open bays, usually avoiding lower salinities.
Comments Representative and most northern of seven species of the Family Atherinidae which occur along the Atlantic and Gulf coasts of USA.

Opah
Lampris guttatus

6ft (1.8m)

Identification Body deep, compressed, with white spot on bluish background. Dorsal fin falcate. Pectoral fins long, directed upward. All fins red.
Range and Habitat Circumtropical, pelagic, or more probably, mesopelagic, extending north to Newfoundland in west Atlantic and Alaska in east Pacific.
Comments A rare or seldom encountered fish whose discovery elicits public attention.

Crestfish
Lophotus lacepede

6ft (1.8m)

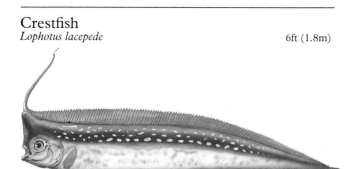

Identification Fins bright red. High dorsal fin lobe on forehead. Body brownish to silvery. Forehead vertical.
Range and Habitat Nearly worldwide; in North America from Florida to Brazil and California. Mesopelagic.
Comments Ink sac present. A curiosity whose stranding always attracts attention. The related unicornfish, *Eumesicthys fiskei*, of both coasts, is much more slender, with the dorsal crest produced far forward of the mouth.

Scalloped ribbonfish
Zu cristatus

6ft (1.8m)

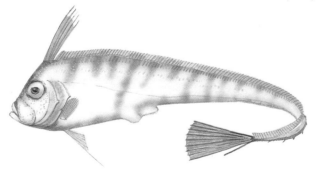

Identification Forehead steep, caudal fin has upper part turned upward and blackish. Silvery, the other fins reddish. Body dark, barred in juveniles; pelvic fins absent in adults.
Range and Habitat Gulf of Mexico and Florida to Cuba, and north California, but probably wide-ranging in mesopelagic zone.

King-of-the-salmon
Trachipterus altivelis

6ft (1.8m)

Identification Body long, tapering to tail, silvery with red fins. Caudal fin upturned.
Range and Habitat Alaska to Chile. Mesopelagic,
Comments Sometimes comes to surface, probably when sick or stressed. Indians believed that this was the king who led the salmons from the sea to the rivers, a legend curiously parallel to king-of-the-herring applied in Europe to the oarfish (below) which supposedly announced the arrival of the herring.

Oarfish
Regalecus glesne

35ft (10.5m)

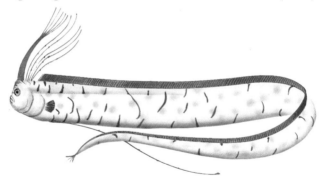

Identification Huge band-like fish, silvery with red fins, the anterior part of dorsal very high with plume-like spines. Pelvic fins long with blade-like membrane.
Range and Habitat Nearly worldwide; in North America reported from Florida and California.
Comments The longest bony fish. Said to reach 500lbs (227kg) and unconfirmed lengths of up to 56ft (17m) have been attributed to it.

Red bream
Beryx decadactylus   24in (61cm)

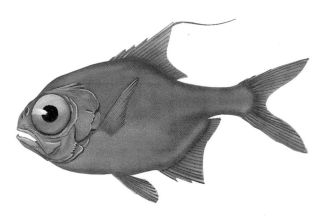

Identification Huge eye. Entirely bright red. The single dorsal spinous in front with first soft ray filamentous. Deep bodied.
Range and Habitat Nova Scotia to Florida, mostly on rough bottom of upper slope waters. Also in eastern Atlantic and Pacific.
Comments Caught by trap and deep-line fishermen. An excellent food fish but too rarely caught in North America for commercial interest.

Squirrelfish
Holocentrus adscensionis   12in (30cm)

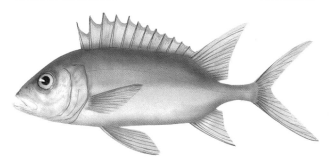

Identification Dull red with yellow to yellow-green spots along outer edge of dorsal fin. Scales spiny, opercular bones spiny.
Range and Habitat North Carolina to Brazil (also in eastern Atlantic) on reefs and rocky bottoms.
Comments Nocturnal. Ten other squirrelfishes or soldierfishes occur along the Atlantic coast of North America mostly along the southeast.

Beardfish
Polymixia lowei   8in (20cm)

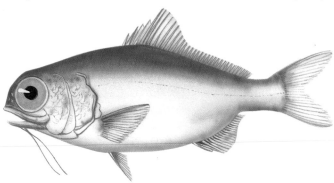

Identification Silvery, with bluish back. Large eye. Single dorsal fin with spines in front. Two long barbels on chin.
Range and Habitat Grand Bank (Newfoundland) to northern South America, mostly on soft bottom on continental or insular slopes to at least 2100ft (640m), occasionally on the shelf.
Comments A primitive spiny-rayed fish, often mentioned in studies of fish phylogeny.

Buckler Dory
Zenopsis conchifera

24in (61cm)

Identification Very compressed fish with big scutes along dorsal and ventral edge of body. Mouth upturned. Dorsal fin spines filamentous. Body silvery, usually with dark spots.
Range and Habitat Nova Scotia to North Carolina, usually on rough bottom.
Comments Related species are esteemed food fishes in Europe and Australia.

Tubesnout
Aulorhynchus flavidus

7in (18cm)

Identification Snout long with small mouth, 24–26 splinter-like spines on back and front of soft dorsal fins.

Range and Habitat Alaska to Baja California, usually in grassy areas or kelp beds.

Comments Like other sticklebacks, male builds and guards nests. Schools during non-breeding season. Sometimes placed in its own Family, Aulorhynchidae.

Threespine stickleback
Gasterosteus aculeatus

4in (10cm)

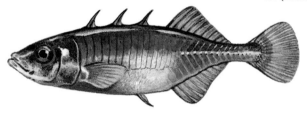

Identification Two separate dorsal spines plus one at front of soft dorsal fin. Usually has bony plates on side. Breeding males have red belly.

Range and Habitat Circumpolar, southward in North America to North Carolina and central California, with extensive fresh water distribution. Usually along shore in seaweed or open grass beds.

Comments An important experimental fish especially in studies of behavior and inheritance. Four other sticklebacks occur littorally in marine waters. The numbers of dorsal spines distinguish them.

Bluespotted cornetfish
Fistularia tabacaria   6ft (1.8m)

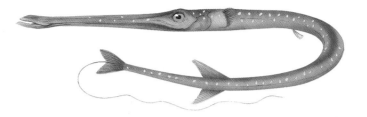

Identification Long snout with terminal mouth, tubular body.
Caudal fin with long central filament. Olive-brown with large whitish
to bluish spots.
Range and Habitat Nova Scotia to Brazil, pelagic but entering
shallow waters; young in bays. Also in eastern Atlantic.
Comments Related red cornetfish, *F. petimba*, also occurs along
southeastern USA. Occasionally taken by anglers.

Trumpetfish
Aulostomus maculatus   36in (91cm)

Identification Long compressed snout, body compressed, greenish
or reddish with black and white markings. Barbel at chin.
Range and Habitat Southeastern USA to South America in grass
beds and around reefs, young offshore.
Comments A commonly photographed and easily observed species.

Slender snipefish
Macroramphosus gracilis

6in (15cm)

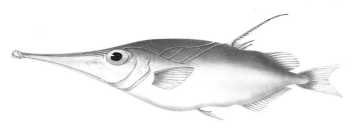

Identification Body compressed, snout long with small terminal mouth. Spine on dorsal fin farther back than pelvic fins, first spine shorter than snout.
Range and Habitat Nearly worldwide in slope waters in low latitudes, from Florida and California southward.
Comments Sometimes very common and fed on by deep-diving yellowfin tuna and dolphins.

Pipehorse
Acentronura dendritica

3in (7.5cm)

Identification Tail curled, prehensile and head slightly bent. Halfway between seahorse and pipefish.
Range and Habitat New Brunswick to Gulf of Mexico. Pelagic but drifting inshore with favorable currents.
Comments Probably common in oceanic drift and sargassum communities.

Lined seahorse
Hippocampus erectus

6in (15cm)

Identification Head bent downward, tail prehensile, curled, and lacking caudal fin. Color variable but has dark lines on neck.
Range and Habitat Nova Scotia to Argentina in shallow coastal areas, usually in cuts and passes with current. Much more common in warm waters. Also in pelagic sargassum community.
Comments A popular aquarium fish. Eggs brooded by male in special pouch. One of four seahorses in North America.

Northern pipefish
Syngnathus fuscus

12in (30cm)

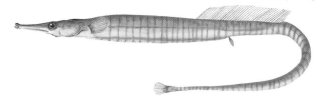

Identification Head and body straight. Tail with caudal fin. Snout moderately long.
Range and Habitat Gulf of St Lawrence to northeastern Florida in coastal waters, bays and inlets, usually in grass beds. Enters fresh water.
Comments This and bay pipefish are representative of 24 pipefish species which occur in North America. All males brood eggs in a chamber on underside of body, the location differing between species.

Bay pipefish
Syngnathus leptorhynchus

9½in (24cm)

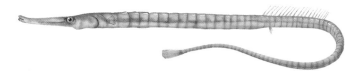

Identification Snout long. Olive-gray or brownish without bands.
Range and Habitat Alaska to Baja California, in bays and sheltered waters. Only pipefish north of California.
Comments Commonly exhibited in aquaria.

Flying gurnard
Dactylopterus volitans

18in (46cm)

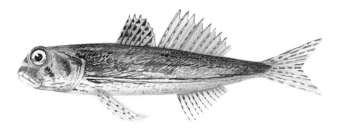

Identification Head armored with posterior spines. Pectoral fins huge, fan-like, with bright barring. Two lower pectoral rays free, finger-like.

Range and Habitat Massachusetts southward, more common in warm water.

Comments An enigmatic fish of uncertain relationships. Commonly exhibited in aquaria.

Smoothhead scorpionfish
Scorpaena calcarata   5in (13cm)

Identification No pit on top of head. Generally pinkish red. Fleshy cirrus above eye. Scales cycloid.
Range and Habitat Southeastern Canada (rare north of North Carolina) to Brazil. In shallow coastal waters and bays, usually in grass beds and around reefs or piers.
Comments Very common. In addition to spotted scorpionfish, 12 other species of *Scorpaena* occur in North American waters.

Spotted scorpionfish
Scorpaena plumieri   12in (30cm)

Identification Pit on top of head. Axil of pectoral fin black with white or yellow spots.
Range and Habitat New York southward in shallow coastal waters.
Comments A lurking species usually resting next to rock and not easily seen. A very similar species occurs in California.

Blackbelly rosefish
Helicolenus dactylopterus

12in (30cm)

Identification Pale red with dusty blotches and a large dark area in rear of spinous dorsal fin.
Range and Habitat Nova Scotia southward below 660ft (200m).
Comments Sometimes confused with species of *Sebastes*. Not currently exploited.

Acadian redfish
Sebastes fasciatus   18in (46cm)

Identification Chin has noticeable projection, usually six to seven anal rays. Generally orange-red.
Range and Habitat Labrador to Gulf of Maine, (possibly Virginia), occurring in shallower waters than deepwater redfish.
Comments All *Sebastes* are live-bearers. This and the deepwater redfish (Atlantic), are harvested collectively as redfish and marketed as ocean perch, mainly as frozen fillets. Very important commercial fish. Largest about 25lbs (11.3kg).

Deepwater redfish
Sebastes mentella   16in (40cm)

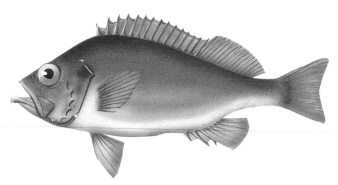

Identification Chin has a noticeable bony protruberance. Eight to ten anal rays. Bright red.
Range and Habitat North Atlantic, from Baffin Island to Scotian shelf, usually deeper than 660ft (200m) except in north.
Comments See Acadian redfish.

Golden redfish
Sebastes norvegicus

20in (51cm)

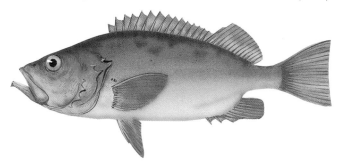

Identification Chin without long protuberance; usually eight anal rays. Generally orange-yellow or golden-yellow.

Range and Habitat North Atlantic, from Gulf of St Lawrence and Newfoundland to Gulf of Maine. Records from farther south may be Acadian redfish.

Comments Long known as *S. marinus*. Rarest of the three species in eastern North America.

Some 62 species of rockfishes occur in Pacific waters of North America. The following 19 species are most commonly encountered, especially from southern Alaska to Oregon.

Pacific ocean perch
Sebastes alutus   20in (51cm)

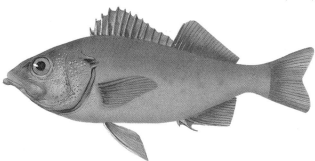

Identification Entirely bright red, often dusky under soft dorsal fin, with a dusky bar at peduncle. Jaw has bony protuberance.
Range and Habitat Alaska to California from shore to 2100ft (640m). Also in northwestern Pacific.
Comments Commercially very important but stocks have declined.

Brown rockfish
Sebastes auriculatus   22in (56cm)

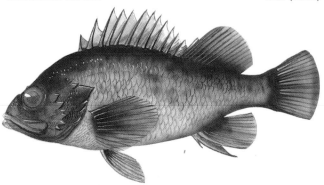

Identification Brown with darker brown blotches. Spinous dorsal fin high. No knob on chin.
Range and Habitat Alaska to Baja California from shore, including inlets, to 420ft (128m).
Comments Primarily a sport fish.

Silvergray rockfish
Sebastes brevispinis   28in (71cm)

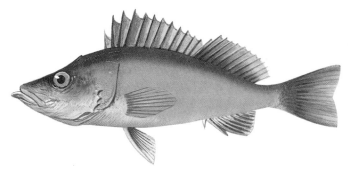

Identification Bluish to silver-gray above, pinkish white below. Chin projects, with bony knob at top.
Range and Habitat Bering Sea to California from shore to 1200ft (366m).
Comments Important commercial fish.

Copper rockfish
Sebastes caurinus   22in (56cm)

Identification Spinous dorsal fin high, largely pale yellow. Head and body coppery brown with extensive pale yellow bars and blotches. Chest white.
Range and Habitat Alaska to California from shore to 600ft (183m).
Comments A very important sport fish, especially in California. World record 5lb 11oz (2.6kg).

Greenstriped rockfish
Sebastes elongatus   15in (38cm)

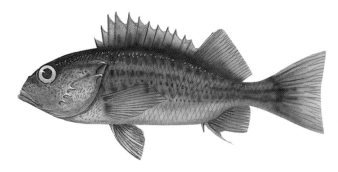

Identification Fins and belly orange-red. Back and upper sides gray-brown with broad pale stripe along lateral line. Green stripes on caudal fin.
Range and Habitat Alaska to Baja California in 200–1320ft (61–402m).
Comments Not highly regarded. Fishermen use them for bait. Some caught with long lines in Alaska.

Yellowtail rockfish
Sebastes flavidus   26in (66cm)

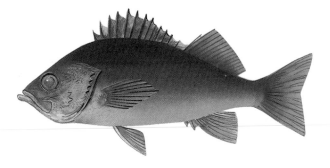

Identification Generally dark brown, almost wine-colored with pale lateral line and whitish belly.
Range and Habitat Alaska to California, often pelagic, occurring from surface to 1800ft (548m).
Comments Commonly caught by trolling and from party boats. Often in schools.

Chillipepper
Sebastes goodei

22in (56cm)

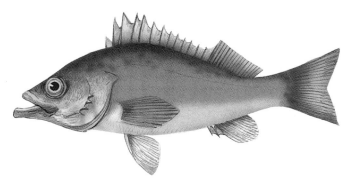

Identification Head, body, and fins pale red; belly white. Lateral line whitish.
Range and Habitat British Columbia to Baja California from surface to 1080ft (329m).
Comments Commercially important in southern part of range. Caught by anglers from party boats.

Shortbelly rockfish
Sebastes jordani

13in (33cm)

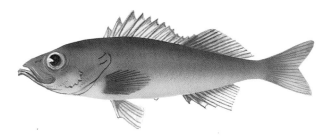

Identification Very slender with projecting lower jaw. Upper body and fins orange-red, lower sides and belly white. Large pale eye.
Range and Habitat British Columbia to Baja California, schooling off bottom in large schools.
Comments An important forage species for fishes, mammals, and seabirds.

Cowcod
Sebastes levis

37in (94cm)

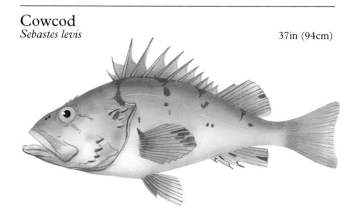

Identification Pale red, sometimes yellowish with high, deeply incised spinous dorsal fins. Usually with brownish bars on upper side. Eye small.
Range and Habitat California to Baja California on deep rocky bottoms from 70–1200ft (21–366m).
Comments An important sport fish. Less important commercially. Reaches 28lb 8oz (13kg).

Quillback
Sebastes maliger

24in (61cm)

Identification Deep body with high, deeply incised spinous dorsal fin. Dark blackish brown with pale yellowish-orange cheeks and belly, with pale yellow extending across spinous dorsal fin onto upper back. Other fins blackish. Eye large.
Range and Habitat Alaska to California on hard bottom from 30–600ft (9–183m).
Comments Important in northern part of range. Popular sport fish caught from party boats. World record 5lb 11oz (2.6kg).

Black rockfish
Sebastes melanops

25in (64cm)

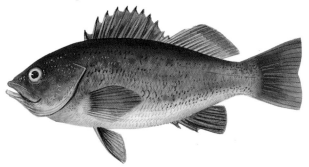

Identification Dark gray becoming black on head and caudal fin.
Range and Habitat Aleutian Islands to California; from surface to
1200ft (366m).
Comments An important sport fish, caught both on bottom and with
trolled gear. A schooling species often feeding near surface. World
record 10lbs (4.6kg).

Vermillion rockfish
Sebastes miniatus

30in (76cm)

Identification Entirely bright red. Iris red. Orangish stripes behind
each eye.
Range and Habitat Southeastern Alaska to Baja California in
100–900ft (33–273m).
Comments A sport fish, young (browner) caught from piers. World
record 11lb 2oz (5kg).

Blue rockfish
Sebastes mystinus

21in (53cm)

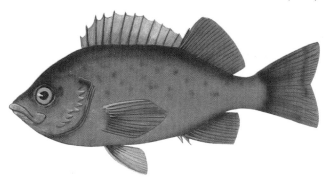

Identification Grayish black except paler below. Fins dark. Jaw shorter than in black rockfish and eye larger.
Range and Habitat Alaska to Baja California from surface to 18,100ft (5517m). A schooling species living off the bottom.
Comments Popular sport fish. Alaskan population may be separate species.

China rockfish
Sebastes nebulosus

17in (43cm)

Identification Blackish brown with yellow stripe from the dorsal spine to lateral line and back to tail. Cheeks and chest yellowish.
Range and Habitat Alaska to California on rocky reefs in 100–420ft (30–128m).
Comments Reputed to be one of the best eating of the rockfishes. Esteemed by orientals, hence the name.

Bocaccio
Sebastes paucispinis   36in (91cm)

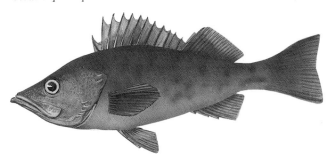

Identification Entirely brick-red, darker above and on fins (except spinous dorsal). Rather slender with large oblique mouth, and projecting chin. Iris dark.
Range and Habitat Alaska to Baja California on rocky and open bottoms.
Comments Commercially harvested in south, caught by anglers throughout range. World record 21lb 4oz (9.6kg).

Canary rockfish
Sebastes pinniger   30in (76cm)

Identification Orangish overall, mottled gray-brown on head and upper body. Iris dark.
Range and Habitat Alaska to Baja California on hard bottom from 100–1200ft (30–366m).
Comments A schooling species commercially important because of high flesh quality. A popular sport fish. World record 10lbs (4.5kg).

Rosy rockfish
Sebastes rosaceus

14in (36cm)

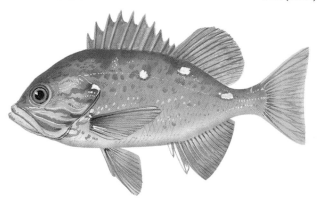

Identification Reddish above becoming more yellow below with four to five well-marked white ovals along upper back.
Range and Habitat Washington to Baja California to 420ft (128m).
Comments Sport fish.

Yelloweye rockfish
Sebastes ruberrimus

36in (91cm)

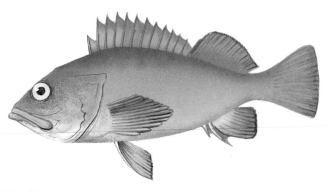

Identification Bright red except white chest and belly, with yellowish tinge on flanks. Bright yellow iris. Ridge of spines above eye.
Range and Habitat Alaska to Baja California on rough bottom in 100-1800ft (30–548m).
Comments Important sport and commercial fish. World record 21lb 4oz (9.6kg). Known as red snapper and marketed under that name in California but this designation is illegal in interstate commerce.

Stripetail rockfish
Sebastes saxicola

15in (38cm)

Identification Projecting lower jaw with knob at tip. Pinkish red overall with yellowish dorsal, caudal, and anal fin. Caudal fin has green streaks. Eye large, pale.
Range and Habitat Alaska to Baja California in offshore waters on muddy bottom in 150–1400ft (46–427m).
Comments Taken by long lines and trawls but too small to be of commercial value.

Shortspine thornyhead
Sebastolobus alascanus

30in (76cm)

Identification Bright red with black blotch toward rear of spinous dorsal and smaller dark area between first two spines. Eye large, dark, top of head very spiny.
Range and Habitat Bering Sea to Baja California in 60–4800ft (18–1463m).
Comments Caught commercially in trawls and traps and in lines but most are too small to be of importance.

Northern searobin
Prionotus carolinus   15in (38cm)

Identification Like all species of *Prionotus*, lower three pectoral rays free, finger-like. Rest of pectoral very long, blackish. Spinous dorsal has black blotch between spines 4–5. Head armored.
Range and Habitat New Brunswick to Florida in shallow coastal waters.
Comments Usually regarded with disdain by fishermen; bait stealers.

Striped searobin
Prionotus evolans   18in (46cm)

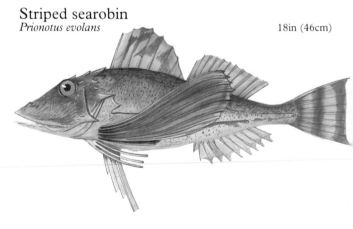

Identification Body tan with two blackish stripes. Pectoral fin very long, its inner surface blackish.
Range and Habitat Nova Scotia to Florida.
Comments This and the northern searobin are representative of 13 species of *Prionotus* and four of *Bellator* which occur in North America and it is the most northern in distribution. Taken by fishermen: world record 3lb 6oz (1.6kg).

Sablefish
Anoplopoma fimbria

40in (1m)

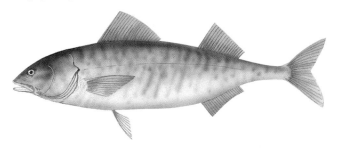

Identification Dark gray to brownish black (generally the blackest fish caught). Paler below with two widely separated dorsal fins.
Range and Habitat North Pacific, along coast from Bering Sea to Baja California, usually below 1200ft (366m).
Comments Important commercially, but rather soft-fleshed. Most are exported. Usually smoked in Canada. Reaches at least 126lbs (57kg). Catches in Bering Sea have reached 16,000 tons (17,000 tonnes).

Skilfish
Erilepis zonifer

70in (1.8m)

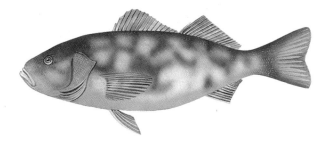

Identification Two dorsal fins contiguous. Dark gray to black with whitish blotches.
Range and Habitat North Pacific, along coast from Bering Sea to California, mostly in deep waters but young taken near surface.
Comments Known to reach 200lbs (91kg) and is reputed to be much larger, but of limited commercial value at present.

Kelp greenling
Hexagrammos decagrammus   21in (53cm)

Identification Dorsal fins joined but with deep notch between
spinous and soft portions. Dark gray with small reddish-brown spots.
Five lateral lines.
Range and Habitat Alaska to California in rocky coastal areas from
short to about 150ft (46m).
Comments An important sport fish both for anglers and spear
fishermen. World record 2lb 12oz (1.2kg).

Rock greenling
Hexagrammos lagocephalus   24in (61cm)

Identification Like kelp greenling but with large cirrus above eye.
Body brown with red marbling, especially in males. Dorsal fins
contiguous.
Range and Habitat Bering Sea to California on high energy rocky
coasts.
Comments Caught from the shore by surf casters.

Lingcod
Ophidon elongatus   5ft (1.5m)

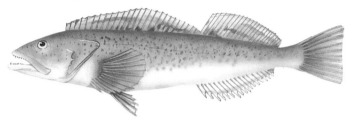

Identification Brown-gray with darker freckling and mottling. Long front dorsal fin. Mouth oblique. Slender. Teeth large.
Range and Habitat Alaska to Baja California in bays and coastal waters but entering deep water.
Comments Commercial and sport fish. World record 64lbs (29kg) but 70lbs (32kg) fish have been landed.

Painted greenling
Oxylebius pictus   10in (25cm)

Identification Pale brown usually with dark reddish bars across body.
Range and Habitat Alaska to Baja California on rocky shores. Common intertidally.
Comments Popular with divers. A commonly photographed fish.

Atka mackerel
Pleurogrammus monopterygius

19½in (49.5cm)

Identification Dorsal fin without notch between spines and rays.
Dark grayish brown with broad, alternately dark and pale bars on
sides. Caudal forked.
Range and Habitat North Pacific, on coast from Bering Sea to
California from near shore to 400ft (122m).
Comments A good food fish, most commonly caught in Alaska.

Longspine combfish
Zaniolepis latipinnis

12in (30cm)

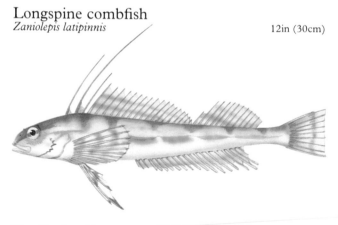

Identification First two dorsal spines mostly free, filamentous,
second largest. Dark bar from eye to snout. Brownish with darker
blotches. Scales sandpapery.
Range and Habitat British Columbia to Baja California in
120–660ft (37–200m).

Sea raven
Hemitripterus americanus   25in (64cm)

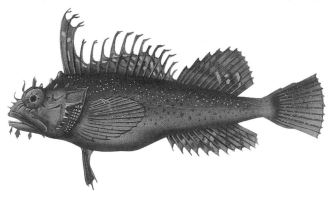

Identification Spines in first dorsal fin separate, with fleshy tabs, appearing tattered, largely separate from soft dorsal. Skin prickly.
Range and Habitat Southern Labrador to Chesapeake Bay on rocky bottom from the shore usually to about 350ft (107m).
Comments Used as lobster bait and as laboratory animal. Swallows water and air when captured to swell the abdomen. Exhibited in public aquaria. A closely related species occurs in Pacific.

Grubby
Myoxocephalus aeneus   7in (18cm)

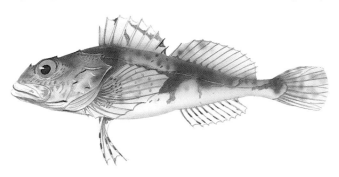

Identification Various shades of brown; dark saddle below first half of spinous dorsal fin, two saddles below soft dorsal. No scales on body.
Range and Habitat Southern Labrador to New Jersey in estuaries and along the coast, tolerant of changing salinities.
Comments Fishermen regard it as a pest, a bait stealer.

Longhorn sculpin
Myoxocephalus octodecemspinosus   18in (46cm)

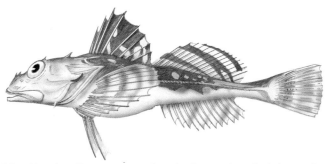

Identification Upper preopercular spine long, unbranched. A row of plate-like scales along lateral line. Dark olive to brown with pale cross bars on fin and blotches on body, whitish on belly.
Range and Habitat Shore waters from Gulf of St Lawrence to Virginia, moving to deeper water during summer in south.
Comments Processed into fish meal in some areas but generally regarded as trash fish. Exhibited in public aquaria.

Great sculpin
Myoxocephalus polyacanthocephalus   30in (76cm)

Identification Upper preopercular spine long, unbranched. Scales few, embedded, not obvious.
Range and Habitat Bering Sea to Washington on soft bottom from the shore to slope waters.
Comments Common and often caught in intracoastal zone. Exhibited in aquaria.

Shorthorn sculpin
Myoxocephalus scorpius   36in (91cm)

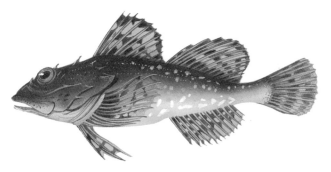

Identification Dark greenish-brown, yellowish below. Males have
pale spots. Upper preopercular spine shorter than next. Row of spiny
scales both above and below lateral line. Six spines on top of head.
Range and Habitat Arctic to New York from shore to 360ft (110m);
also in eastern Atlantic.
Comments Sometimes stranded on very low tides. Caught but
disdained by anglers. Used for lobster bait.

Sailfin sculpin
Nautichthys oculofasciatus   8in (20cm)

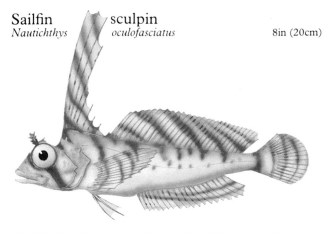

Identification Spinous dorsal fin very high. Pale brown with dark
brown bar through eye and across cheek. Fins have brown barring.
Body sandpapery.
Range and Habitat Alaska to California from shore to 360ft
(110m).
Comments Exhibited in public aquaria.

Rosylip sculpin
Ascelichthys rhodorus

6in (15cm)

Identification Pelvic fins absent. No scales. Dorsal fins broadly joined, first lower than second. Dark brown, often with red lips.
Range and Habitat Southeastern Alaska to California, mainly in tidepools on high energy rocky coasts. Can be found under rocks at low tide.
Comments A common tidepool species. The only sculpin without pelvic fins.

Sharpnose sculpin
Clinocottus acuticeps

7in (18cm)

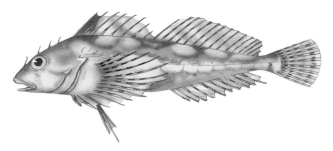

Identification Snout pointed; body without scales, brown with darker saddles, paler below. Dorsal fin brown behind first spine. Inner edge of pelvic broadly joined to belly.
Range and Habitat Alaska to California in shallow water in many habitats including estuaries but most common in rocky and grassy areas.
Comments Abundant in intertidal areas.

Mosshead sculpin
Clinocottus globiceps   7½in (19cm)

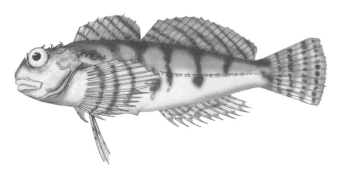

Identification Snout very blunt. Body without scales. Many hair-like filaments on top of head and along front part of lateral line. Dark brown with obscure darker bars. Fins have dark cross banding.
Range and Habitat Southeastern Alaska to California in tidepools.
Comments Easily found at low-tide under mats of seaweed around exposed tidepools.

Red Irish lord
Hemilepidotus hemilepidotus   20in (51cm)

Identification Swath of scales along back and another on flank below lateral line. Generally reddish with both blackish and whitish blotches, usually with four dark saddles on back.
Range and Habitat Bering Sea to California, from shore to about 100ft (30m).
Comments Caught by anglers. Regarded as a good-flavored fish.

Buffalo sculpin
Enophrys bison   14½in (37cm)

Identification Long, strong preopercular and a strong lower spine
pointing downward. Large plate-like scales on lateral line. Dark saddle
under each dorsal fin.
Range and Habitat Gulf of Alaska to California from shore to 65ft
(20m).
Comments When disturbed, opens gill cover to display the
prominent armor. The sculpins described are representative of 96
marine species occurring in cold coastal waters, most of them in the
North Pacific.

Atlantic poacher
Leptagonus decagonus   9in (23cm)

Identification Two dorsal fins present. Body plated. Anus between
pelvic fins. Barbels along lower jaw.
Range and Habitat Arctic Ocean to Strait of Belle Isle and the
Newfoundland banks in moderate depths of 80–1320ft (24–402m).
Comments A truly Arctic species.

Alligatorfish
Aspidophoroides monopterygius   7in (18cm)

Identification Spinous dorsal fin absent, back smooth (spiny in Atlantic poacher). Two dark bands between pectoral and dorsal fins.
Range and Habitat Labrador to New Jersey in 66–660ft (20–200m).
Comments A little-known species, which is preyed upon by cods and other commercially important fishes.

Kelp poacher
Agonomalus mozinoi   3½in (9cm)

Identification Mottled bright red and brown with fleshy flap on snout; fins large. Dorsal fins high, mostly bright red.
Range and Habitat British Columbia to California in rocky tidepools and exposed coasts to 35ft (11m).
Comments An attractive and interesting species that should attract marine aquarists. In addition to the poachers described above, 24 other Pacific and one other Atlantic species occur in North American coastal waters.

Lumpfish
Cyclopterus lumpus

24in (61cm)

Identification Greenish gray with rows of tubercles down back and three other rows along the side. Pelvic fins form a suction disk. Fanlike pectoral fins.
Range and Habitat Hudson Bay and Labrador to Middle Atlantic states, also in eastern Atlantic. From rocky shores and floating mats of seaweed to 1090ft (332m).
Comments Roe used for caviar. A food fish in Europe but not in North America, although it is reputed to have a good flavor.

Inquiline snailfish
Liparis inquilinus

2¾in (7cm)

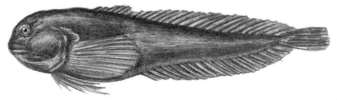

Identification Skin without scales or tubercles, but with prickles.
Range and Habitat Gulf of St Lawrence to North Carolina from shore to 320ft (97m).
Comments Lives in the mantle cavity of the giant scallop, *Placopectin magellanicus*, which they leave at night to feed. Up to eight have been reported from a single scallop. They apparently spawn once and die. The lumpfish and inquiline snailfish are representative of 46 species of the Family Cyclopteridae occurring in North American coastal waters, most of them in the Pacific.

Common snook
Centropomus undecimalis   4ft (1.2m)

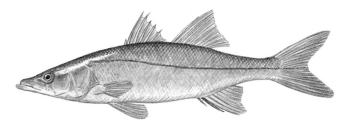

Identification Silvery-sided with black lateral line which extends to edge of caudal fin. Pelvic fin pale.
Range and Habitat South Carolina and Gulf of Mexico to Brazil, in estuarine and coastal waters and entering fresh water.
Comments A prized sport and food fish, prohibited from commercial sale in Florida. World record 53lb 10oz (24.3kg). Three related species, all smaller, occur in Florida.

White perch
Morone americana   19in (48cm)

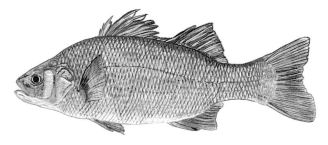

Identification Silvery with darker back. Caudal fin shallowly forked.
Range and Habitat Gulf of St Lawrence to North Carolina mainly in estuaries and fresh water but entering coastal marine waters. Anadromous, with landlocked populations.
Comments A minor sport and food fish, usually prepared as a pan fish. World record 4lb 12oz (2.2kg) but known to reach 6lbs (2.7kg).

Striped bass
Morone saxatilis

6ft (1.8m)

Identification Dark greenish above, silvery on sides with bold black stripes along sides.
Range and Habitat Gulf of St Lawrence to northeastern Florida and Gulf of Mexico in coastal waters, bays and estuaries, running up rivers. Some permanent freshwater populations. Introduced to Pacific coast where it is now established from British Columbia to Baja California. Widely introduced elsewhere.
Comments A premier food and sport fish. World record 78lb 8oz (35.6kg) but known to reach 125lbs (57kg). Atlantic stocks are seriously depleted.

Giant sea bass
Stereolepis gigas

7½ft (2.3m)

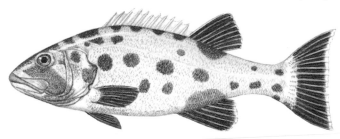

Identification Generally dark brown, young are spotted and blotched. Caudal fin only slightly concave. Spinous dorsal fin low.
Range and Habitat California and northwestern Mexico on rocky bottom with a lot of surge.
Comments Important sport fish but stocks depleted. World record 563lb 8oz (225.6kg).

Wreckfish
Polyprion americanus   7ft (2.1m)

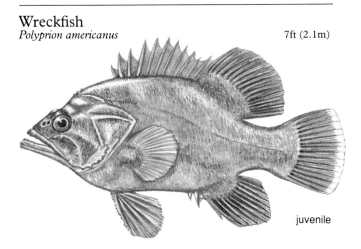

juvenile

Identification Dark grayish-brown, juveniles blotched. Caudal fin rounded. Heads with bony bumps above eye and nape and with a pronounced bony ridge across opercle. Lower jaw projecting.
Range and Habitat Southeastern Canada to northern Florida around rocky ledges and wrecks in deep water, 200–2000ft (61–610m). Also in temperate parts of other oceans except eastern Pacific.
Comments Now heavily fished off southeastern USA but stocks are declining. World record sports catch 106lb 4oz (48.2kg).

Black sea bass
Centropristis striata   24in (61cm)

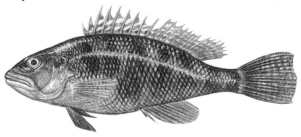

Identification Males bluish-black with large white patches on head and three-lobed caudal fin. Females brown with paler blotches and rounded caudal fin. Dimorphism less marked in Gulf of Mexico.
Range and Habitat New Brunswick to northern Florida and northern Gulf of Mexico in shallow water usually on rough bottoms or around harbors and rock jetties.
Comments Popular with anglers. World record 9lb 8oz (4.3kg).

Rock hind
Epinephelus adscensionis   24in (61cm)

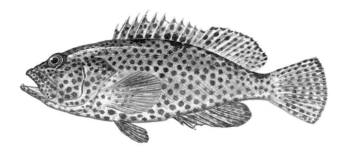

Identification Brownish with large reddish-brown spots that are
distinctly larger toward belly. Two blackish saddles on back.
Range and Habitat Massachusetts to Brazil along the coast on rocky
ledges and reefs, including coral reefs.
Comments A food and sport fish. World record 2lb 5oz (1kg). All
species of *Epinephelus* and *Mycteroperca* show sex reversal, the very
largest individuals of each species being male.

Red hind
Epinephelus guttatus   24in (61cm)

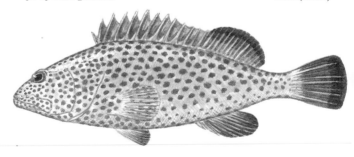

Identification Spots redder than in rock hind and no larger on belly
than on sides. No saddles on back. Caudal, soft dorsal and anal fins
with outer third blackish.
Range and Habitat North Carolina to Brazil, especially common
around reefs.
Comments A food and sport fish. World record 2lb 14oz (1.3kg).

Coney
Epinephelus fulvus   12in (30cm)

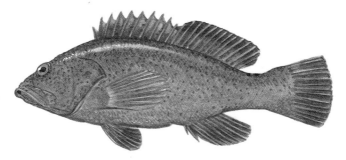

Identification Several color phases: yellow, dark reddish-brown, bicolored, dark brown or reddish above, tan below. All phases have small blue spots on body, two black spots at chin and two on top of caudal peduncle.
Range and Habitat Florida to Brazil especially around coral reefs.
Comments Commonly exhibited in public aquaria. A minor food and sport fish.

Jewfish
Epinephelus itajara   8ft (2.4m)

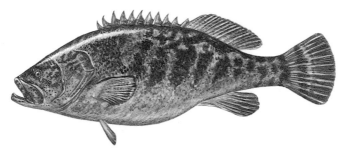

Identification Pale brown with irregular dark bands. Young with many black spots. Spinous dorsal fin low.
Range and Habitat Gulf of Mexico and eastern Florida to Brazil in shallow water around grassbeds and mangroves and especially around wrecks and coral reefs.
Comments A tackle-busting game fish, not often used for food. Largest grouper, reliably reported to reach 1000lbs (454kg). World record 680lbs (308kg).

Red grouper
Epinephelus morio

42in (1.1m)

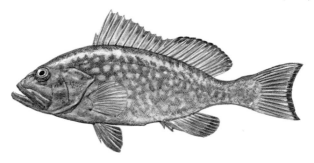

Identification Dark mahogany brown; mouth lining orangish. Spinous dorsal fin high with even edge.
Range and Habitat Massachusetts to Brazil in deeper water 80–400ft (24–122m).
Comments An important commercial species but stocks are depleted. World record sports catch 37lb 8oz (17kg).

Warsaw grouper
Epinephelus nigritus

6ft (1.8m)

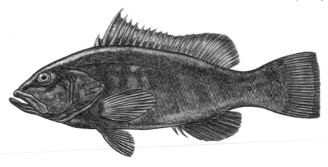

Identification Dark brown overall with very long second spine in dorsal fin and large rear nostril. Young have yellow tail and dark saddle on caudal peduncle.
Range and Habitat Massachusetts to Brazil usually in deep rocky outcrops and pinnacles in 300–1000ft (91–305m).
Comments A giant species reaching 580lbs (263kg). World record sports catch 436lb 12oz (198kg). Stocks have been depleted.

Nassau grouper
Epinephelus striatus 36in (91cm)

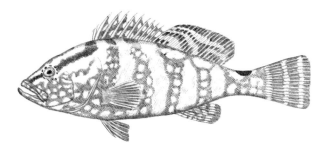

Identification Pale brown with dark saddle on caudal peduncle, black spots around eye and dark brown stripe from snout to dorsal fin. Body often with dark bars.
Range and Habitat North Carolina to Brazil in shallow coastal waters and around reefs and cuts.
Comments An important food and game fish but stocks have been seriously depleted. World record 27lb 8oz (12.5kg) but known to reach 55lbs (25kg).

Scamp
Mycteroperca phenax 24in (61cm)

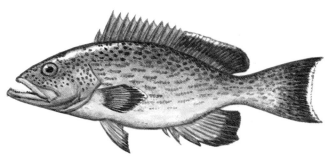

Identification Completely covered with dark brown or brassy spots that may form lines or blotches. Caudal fin with rays extending as short filaments in large adults.
Range and Habitat Massachusetts to Venezuela in open coastal waters.
Comments Food and sport fish. World record catch 23lb 2oz (10.5kg).

Yellowfin grouper
Mycteroperca venenosa   36in (91cm)

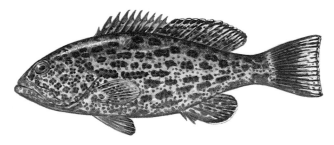

Identification Large, horizontally ovate, dark blotches, red in some fish. Outer part of pectoral fin dull to bright yellow.
Range and Habitat Florida to Brazil around reefs and rocky slopes in clear water. Not entering bays.
Comments A sport fish, but this is one of our most consistently ciguatoxic fishes and should never be eaten. World record 34lb 6oz (15.4kg).

Broomtail grouper
Mycteroperca xenarcha   4ft (1.2m)

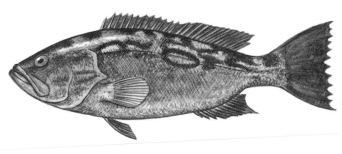

Identification Caudal fin with rays extending out from edge of fin, hence the name. Pale brown with large darker blotches, usually ovate.
Range and Habitat California to Peru usually in shallow water.
Comments A food and sport fish reputedly reaching 200lbs (91kg); world record 60lbs (27kg). Some 26 groupers, *Epinephelus* and *Mycteroperca* occur in North American coastal waters of which the species described are representative.

Kelp bass
Paralabrax clathratus   28½in (72cm)

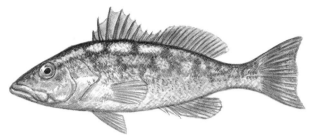

Identification Olive-brown with ovate pale blotches. Third dorsal spine about equal to fourth.
Range and Habitat Washington to Baja California in shallow waters, usually in and around kelp beds.
Comments Sport fish, taken both by anglers and spear fishermen. A good food fish. Reaches 14lb 8oz (6.6 kg). Three other species of *Paralabrax* occur in California.

Bigeye
Priacanthus arenatus   12in (30cm)

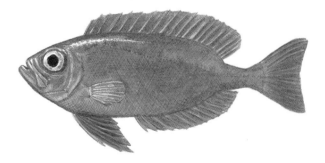

Identification Orange-red with long pelvic fin which is blackish or black-tipped. Eye very large.
Range and Habitat Nova Scotia to Argentina; also in eastern Atlantic. Nocturnal usually on shallow rough bottoms and around reefs and cuts.
Comments Taken by anglers and sometimes marketed as snapper. World record 2lb 8oz (1.1kg).

Twospot cardinalfish
Apogon pseudomaculatus   4½in (11cm)

Identification Entirely red with two black spots, one under soft
dorsal, the other on caudal peduncle. Soft dorsal, anal and caudal fins
with black tips in smaller fish.
Range and Habitat Banks off southeastern Canada to Brazil in
coastal waters including clear-water harbors and bays, usually around
walls, pilings, or other areas with hard relief.
Comments This and the conchfish represent the Apogonidae, of
which 19 species occur in North America, all but one in Atlantic
waters. Cardinalfishes are popular aquarium fishes and the males
brood the eggs orally.

Conchfish
Astrapogon stellatus   2½in (6.4cm)

Identification Largely brownish with long, blackish pelvic fins which
reach well back of anal fin.
Range and Habitat Florida and Caribbean region in shallow waters.
Comments Lives in the mantle cavity of living conch.

Ocean whitefish
Caulolatilus princeps   40in (1m)

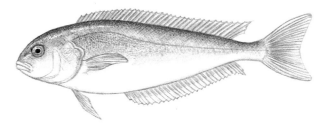

Identification Elongate with thick lips and a long unnotched dorsal fin. Caudal fin shallowly forked. Generally brownish with pale yellow and blue in fins.
Range and Habitat British Columbia to Peru on rocky reefs and rises usually between 33–300ft (10–91m).
Comments A good eating fish. Four additional species of *Caulolatilus* occur in Atlantic waters in the southeastern USA.

Tilefish
Lopholatilus chamaeleonticeps   42in (1.1m)

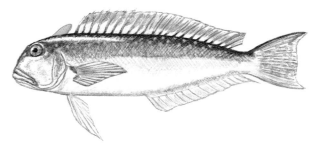

Identification Fleshy tab on top of head. Body tan with many yellow spots.
Range and Habitat Southeastern Canada to Guyana in deep shelf and upper slope waters.
Comments Reaches 50lbs (22.7kg). An important commercial food fish and locally important as a sport fish.

Bluefish
Pomatomus saltatrix

45in (1.1m)

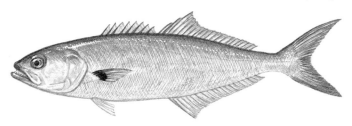

Identification Silvery with dark back; dark blotch at base of pectoral fin. Soft dorsal and anal fins covered with scales and with a long base. Large mouth with strong teeth.

Range and Habitat New Brunswick and Nova Scotia to Florida. Also in Venezuela and other parts of the world. A coastal pelagic species, migrating in large schools. Young in bays and sheltered waters.

Comments Bluefish commonly follow menhaden (p.40) and other schooling forage fishes. An important food and sport fish. World record 31lb 12oz (14.4kg). Known to bite people when schools move into bathing areas.

Cobia
Rachycentron canadum

6ft (1.8m)

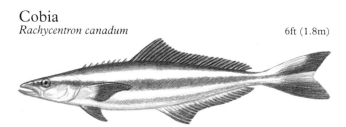

Identification Usually rather dark with darker stripe along midsides, this more prominent in smaller fish. Fins blackish. Head broad and flattened. Very low spinous dorsal fin, the spines separate.

Range and Habitat Nova Scotia to Argentina but worldwide in warm waters although not on Pacific coast. Pelagic, entering coastal waters, even into harbors and coastal canals.

Comments An excellent game fish, esteemed as a smoked fish. Reaches 150lbs (68kg). World record 135lb 7oz (61.5kg).

Sharksucker
Echeneis naucrates   36in (91cm)

Identification Broad black stripe with narrow white stripe above and below. Color otherwise changeable. Suction disk on head.
Range and Habitat Worldwide. In area from Nova Scotia southward and in California. Pelagic but entering protected coastal waters and even following hosts into fresh water in some areas.
Comments Eight species of remora are known and all occur in North America. This species is more often seen swimming free than any other species and it attaches to many kinds of fishes and sea turtles.

Remora
Remora remora   30in (76cm)

Identification Completely brownish black. Pectoral fin flexible.
Range and Habitat Worldwide. Pelagic in areas from Nova Scotia and California southward.
Comments Attaches mainly to sharks but will attach to fish and turtles.

African pompano
Alectis ciliaris

42in (1.1m)

Identification Dorsal profile sharply angled. Spinous dorsal with filamentous rays, usually broken in adults. Scutes alongside caudal peduncle. Caudal fin lunate.
Range and Habitat Worldwide in warm waters. In North America from Massachusetts southward. Pelagic, usually offshore.
Comments An important sport fish. World record 49lbs (22.2kg). Known to be ciguatoxic.

Blue runner
Caranx crysos

20in (51cm)

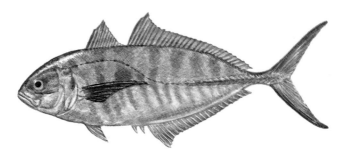

Identification Adults rather dark with black opercular spot. Short arch to lateral line. Rear part of lateral line scuted.
Range and Habitat Atlantic Ocean. In North America from Gulf of St Lawrence southward. Pelagic, but common in coastal waters.
Comments A food and sport fish, also used for bait. World record 7lbs (3.2kg). Referred to by many icthyologists as *Carangoides*.

Crevalle jack
Caranx hippos

5ft (1.5m)

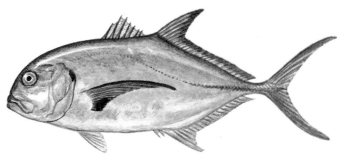

Identification Black spot on opercle and on pectoral fin. Forehead very steep. Lateral line scuted along caudal peduncle.
Range and Habitat Nova Scotia to Uruguay. Pelagic but common in harbors, bays and estuaries.
Comments Sport fish. World record 54lb 7oz (24.7kg). An important food fish elsewhere but little used. Seven other species of *Caranx* (with broad seas) occur in North America.

Pilotfish
Naucrates ductor

27in (68.5cm)

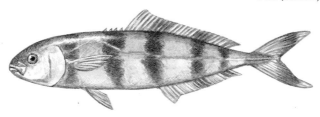

Identification Caudal peduncle without scutes. Fins and body crossed by five to seven blackish bands. Caudal fin lobes white.
Range and Habitat Nova Scotia and British Columbia southward but nearly worldwide. Pelagic.
Comments Usually occurs under rafts of seaweed or in association with large pelagic fish, sharks and rays.

Atlantic moonfish
Selene setapinnis

12in (30cm)

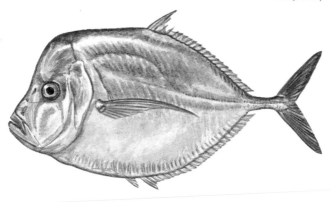

Identification Forehead nearly vertical, its outline somewhat concave. Soft dorsal and anal fins low with no elongate rays. No scutes on caudal peduncle. Body extremely compressed, silvery.
Range and Habitat Nova Scotia to Uruguay in coastal waters. Also in eastern Atlantic.
Comments A schooling species.

Lookdown
Selene vomer

12in (30cm)

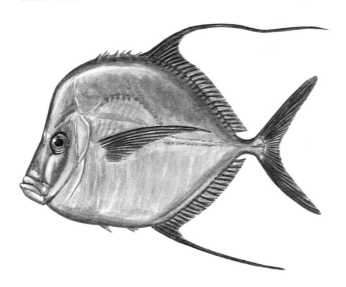

Identification Forehead nearly vertical, profile straight. Soft dorsal and anal fins with anterior rays very long, forming a high fin lobe. No scutes on caudal peduncle. Body extremely compressed. Silvery.
Range and Habitat Nova Scotia to Uruguay in coastal waters. Also in eastern Atlantic.
Comments Oceanic in large schools. A minor sport fish, world record 3lb 11oz (1.7kg).

Greater amberjack
Seriola dumerili

5ft (1.5m)

Identification No scutes on caudal peduncle. Brown stripe from snout tip to dorsal-fin origin. Front lobe of dorsal and anal fin only slightly elevated. Often with olive-yellow strip along side.
Range and Habitat Nearly worldwide in warm waters; in North America from Nova Scotia southward. Pelagic but entering coastal waters around reefs, wrecks and rocky pinnacles.
Comments An important food and sport fish though its flesh is rather strong, often wormy, and sometimes ciguatoxic. World record 155lb 10oz (71kg) but reaches at least 176lbs (80kg).

Almaco jack
Seriola falcatus

5ft (1.5m)

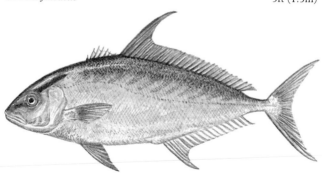

Identification No scutes on caudal peduncle. Brownish stripe from snout tip almost to dorsal fin. Front lobes of dorsal and anal fin high, the fin margins deeply falcate.
Range and Habitat Worldwide in warm waters. In North America from Massachusetts and California southward. Pelagic but entering near-shore waters.
Comments A food and sport fish, the Pacific population reaching a larger size. World records: Atlantic 62lb 12oz (28.5kg); Pacific 132lbs (60kg).

Yellowtail
Seriola lalandi 5ft (1.5m)

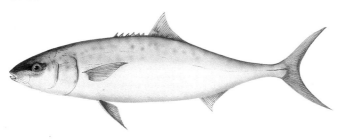

Identification Like greater amberjack (p124) but stripe from snout becomes obscure behind eye. Yellow stripe along sides. Caudal fin, and often the other fins, yellowish.
Range and Habitat Nearly worldwide in warm waters. In North America from British Columbia southward. Pelagic, congregating around rocky islets, kelp beds and exposed rocky shores.

Florida pompano
Trachinotus carolinus 25in (64cm)

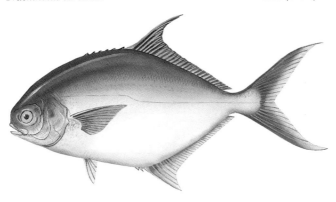

Identification Deep silvery body, first dorsal fin has very short (barely visible) spines. Dorsal and anal fin lobes high. No scutes on caudal peduncle.
Range and Habitat Massachusetts to Brazil in shallow coastal waters including bays, inlets, and estuaries.
Comments A premier food and sport fish: broiled pompano is a restaurant speciality. Attempts to culture the species in ponds have not been profitable. World record 8lb 1oz (3.7kg).

Permit
Trachinotus falcatus

45in (1.1m)

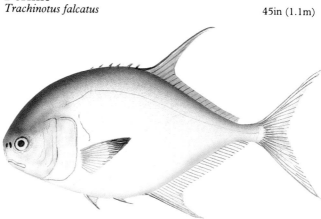

Identification Very similar to pompano but body deeper and fin shorter (16–19 rays vs 22–27).
Range and Habitat Massachusetts to Brazil in open coastal waters.
Comments Primarily a sport fish. World record 51lbs (23kg).

Rough scad
Trachurus lathami

16in (40cm)

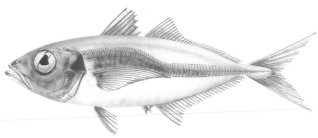

Identification Eye very large. Lateral line with large scutes over entire length. No finlets.
Range and Habitat Banks off Nova Scotia to Venezuela; in schools in coastal waters.
Comments Six similar species of the genera *Decapterus, Selar,* and *Trachurus* occur along North American coasts. The previous 12 species are representative of 37 species of the jack family, Carangidae, which occur in North America, all in warm waters.

Roosterfish
Nematistius pectoralis   4ft (1.2m)

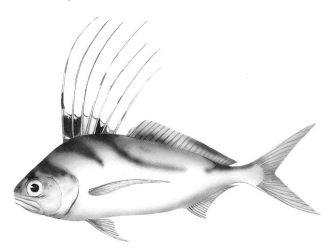

Identification Spinous dorsal with each spine filamentous, extending far beyond the fin membrane. Two dark stripes extending from base of dorsal fin down and along side.
Range and Habitat California to Peru. Pelagic but coming close to shore both on reefs and open beaches.
Comments A good sport fish related to the dolphins and the jacks. World record 114lbs (51.7kg).

Dolphin
Coryphaena hippurus   6¾ft (2.1m)

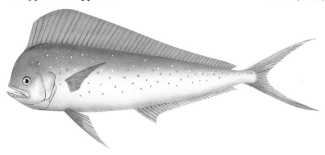

Identification Males (called bulls) have forehead nearly vertical (rounded in females). Single dorsal fin begins above eye. Body bluish above, bright yellow on sides with blue or greenish fins.
Range and Habitat Worldwide. In North America from Nova Scotia and Washington southward. Pelagic, oceanic, but young drift into bays with seaweed.
Comments Like to feed under islands of seaweed, drift lines, and logs. A prized food and sport fish (sold as maji maji in Hawaii and in restaurants with an island cuisine). World record 87lbs (39.5kg). A second species, the pompano dolphin, occurs in much the same area. It is smaller and more snake-like in its habits.

Cubera snapper
Lutjanus cyanopterus   5ft (1.5m)

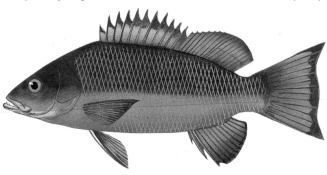

Identification Almost entirely dark grayish-brown. Teeth on vomer form a simple crescent.
Range and Habitat Nova Scotia to Brazil, from cuts and inlets to ledges in deeper water (180ft (55m)).
Comments A bullish sport fish, but flesh may be ciguatoxic. World record 121lb 8oz (55.1kg). Grows larger.

Gray snapper
Lutjanus griseus   24in (61cm)

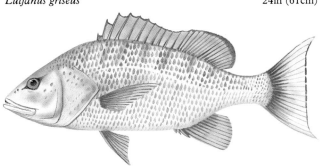

Identification Dark gray with reddish cast. Dark stripe from snout to dorsal fin. Blue line on snout.
Range and Habitat Massachusetts to Brazil from offshore reefs to estuaries, even entering fresh water.
Comments An excellent food and sport fish. World record 18lb 8oz (8.4kg). Widely known in Florida and the Caribbean as the mangrove snapper. A common market fish.

Red snapper
Lutjanus campechanus   36in (91cm)

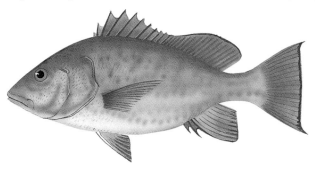

Identification Entirely pale red, whitish below. Anal fin ovate. Spot on side ill-defined, only on small individuals.
Range and Habitat North Carolina to Yucatan, mostly in deeper shelf water but caught from ocean piers in the Carolinas.
Comments Important commercial fish. World record sports catch 46lb 8oz (21.1kg). Fourteen species of *Lutjanus* occur in North America, most on the Atlantic coast, of which the previous three species are representative.

Tripletail
Lobotes surninamensis 42in (1.1m)

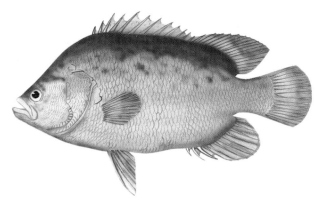

Identification Various shades of brown. Soft dorsal, anal and caudal fins form a three-lobed posterior fin, hence the name. Forehead concave.

Range and Habitat Worldwide in warm waters. In North America from Nova Scotia southward. Pelagic. Commonly into drift entering inshore waters and bays.

Comments A sport fish, though very easily caught. World record 42lb 8oz (19.2kg).

White grunt
Haemulon plumieri   18in (46cm)

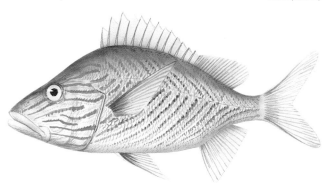

Identification Many narrow blue and yellow stripes on head. Scales above lateral line distinctly larger than those below. Soft dorsal, caudal and anal fins densely scaled.

Range and Habitat Maryland to Brazil in shallow waters, most common in harbors, cuts and in reefs in warm waters.

Comments Representative of 14 species of *Haemulon*, *Anisotremus*, and *Macrolepidotus*, most of which are more southern in distribution. Excellent pan fishes but not entering the commercial trade in any important way. World record 5lb 3oz (2.4kg).

Pigfish
Orthopristis chrysoptera

15in (38cm)

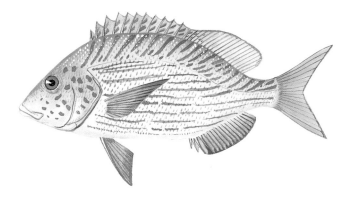

Identification Bluish gray with yellowish spots on most scales. Small mouth.
Range and Habitat New York to southern Gulf of Mexico, rarer in southern part of range except after cold winters. A shallow water inhabitant of grass beds in bays and inlets. Not on reefs.
Comments A good pan fish, commonly caught from shore.

Sheepshead
Archosargus probatocephalus 36in (91cm)

Identification Silvery with bluish, diagonal lines across body.
Range and Habitat Nova Scotia to Brazil in bays and estuaries;
common around pilings, wharfs and seawalls.
Comments Caught by anglers from shore. World record 21lb 4oz
(9.6kg).

Pinfish
Lagodon rhomboides

14in (36cm)

Identification Body with blue and yellow strips with a dark shoulder spot centered on lateral line. Ventral profile a smooth arc.

Range and Habitat Massachusetts to Yucatan in shallow waters, usually in grass beds.

Comments A popular pan fish usually less than 1lb but world record 1lb 6oz (0.6kg).

Scup

Stenotomus chrysops   18in (46cm)

Identification Silvery on sides, dark olive with faint darker bars across body. Blue stripe along base of dorsal fin.
Range and Habitat New Brunswick to Florida in and around harbors and inlets.
Comments A popular pan fish for anglers. Marketed locally. World record 4lb 2oz (1.9kg). The three porgies described (above) are representative of 16 species occurring in warm waters of North America, all but one in the Atlantic.

Spotted seatrout
Cynoscion nebulosus   36in (91cm)

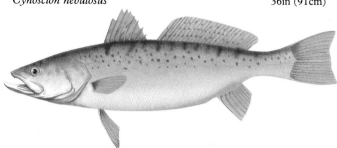

Identification Conspicuous black spots on silvery body. Back bluish.
Lateral line extends across caudal fin. Teeth large, lower jaw
protruding.
Range and Habitat Maryland to Gulf of Mexico, primarily in bays
and inland waterways over grass beds.
Comments An excellent food and sport fish. World record 16lbs
(7.2kg).

Weakfish
Cynoscion regalis   36in (91cm)

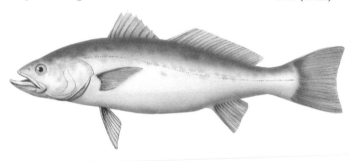

Identification Silvery with bluish or brownish back with many ill-
defined dark spots of different intensity.
Range and Habitat Nova Scotia to Florida in coastal waters,
entering bays.
Comments An important food and sport fish whose stocks have been
seriously depleted. World record 19lb 2oz (8.7kg).

White croaker
Genyonemus lineatus 16¼in (41cm)

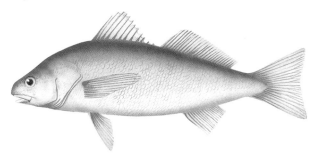

Identification Small blackish spot at base of pectoral fin. Generally silvery with wavy dark lines along scale rows.
Range and Habitat British Columbia to Baja California in schools in shallow waters but recorded at 600ft (183m).
Comments Important food and sport fish. Marketed locally.

Spot
Leiostomus xanthurus 14in (36cm)

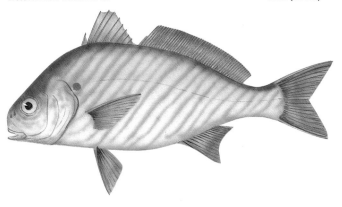

Identification No barbels on chin. Dark brown shoulder spot with narrow, diagonal, dark bands across upperside. Caudal fin forked.
Range and Habitat Massachusetts to northeastern Florida and Gulf of Mexico in bays, inlets, and near-shore waters.
Comments An excellent pan-fried fish, popular with anglers. Often featured as catch-of-the-day in seaside restaurants.

Queenfish
Seriphus politus

12in (30cm)

Identification Silvery with darker back, the two dorsal fins distinctly separated. No barbels. Mouth oblique, terminal.

Range and Habitat Oregon to Baja California in bays and tidal creeks and in harbors.

Comments A schooling species of limited value as a food and sport fish although commonly caught by anglers. The previous seven species are representative of 33 species of drums (Family Sciaenidae) found in North American waters, many of them important as food and sport fishes.

Red goatfish
Mullus auratus

10in (25cm)

Identification Two long barbels at base of chin (as in all goatfishes). Head and body mostly red, somewhat blotched and with two yellow or orangish stripes on side.

Range and Habitat Nova Scotia to northern South America in schools in shelf waters (30–300ft (19–91m)).

Comments Six species of goatfishes occur in North American waters. They differ in color and color pattern and are commonly exhibited in aquaria. Related species are sold in European markets.

Black drum
Pogonias cromis

5½ft (1.7m)

Identification Many short barbels forming a fringe along jaw. Massive head, deep body, with blackish bars on body, best marked in smaller fish.
Range and Habitat Nova Scotia to southern Gulf of Mexico. Also in southwestern Atlantic. Common in bays and tidal creeks.
Comments An important sport fish, fished for by surf casters and shore fishermen using heavy tackle. World record 113lb 1oz (51.3kg). The flesh is strong and coarse and heavily parasitized and so the large fish are generally not eaten.

Red drum
Sciaenops ocellatus

4¾ft (1.5m)

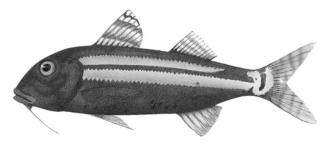

Identification Adults bronzish, juvenile silvery. Mouth inferior. Black spot, or spots often ocellated on caudal peduncle near base of caudal fin. No barbels.
Range and Habitat Massachusetts to southern Gulf of Mexico in bays, inlets, and shore waters.
Comments Popularized by cajun style "blackened" cooking. Stocks depleted. Cultured for stocking. An excellent food fish up to about 13lbs (6kg). World record 94lb 2oz (42.7kg). Also known as spot-tail bass (Carolinas), redfish (Gulf coast) or channel bass.

Opaleye
Girella nigricans

25in (64cm)

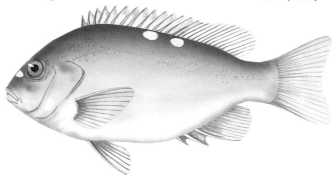

Identification Eye bright blue occasionally greenish. Head rounded, the body ovate. Dark olive-gray usually with two large white spots just below dorsal fin. Caudal fin shallowly forked.
Range and Habitat California to Baja California in intertidal areas.
Comments Taken by small hooks and by spearing. Also fished commercially with nets set to encircle the schools. Largest 13lb 8oz (6kg).

Bermuda chub
Kyphosus sectatrix

30in (76cm)

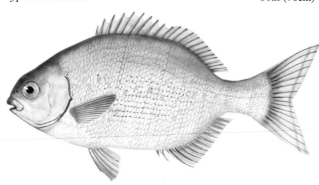

Identification Body bluish-gray with narrow yellow stripes on body and broad yellow stripe below eye. Can change rapidly to a white-spotted pattern.
Range and Habitat Massachusetts to Brazil; pelagic; under drift lines; common in clearwater harbors around pilings and ship hulls.
Comments Can be caught with small hooks but not usually sought by anglers. World record 8lb 11oz (3.9kg). The previous two species represent seven sea chubs, Kyphosidae, known from North America.

Atlantic spadefish
Chaetodipterus faber   36in (91cm)

Identification Very deep body with steep rounded forehead, the soft
dorsal and anal fins have high lobes. Silvery with tan to blackish
bands, these paling at times.
Range and Habitat Massachusetts to Brazil usually in schools in
coastal waters including bays and harbors.
Comments World record 9lb 6oz (4.2kg) but reported to 20lbs
(9kg). A very similar species occurs from California to Peru.

Spotfin butterflyfish
Chaetodon ocellatus   8in (20cm)

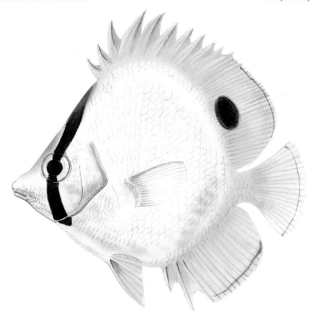

Identification Body disk-shaped, compressed. Silvery with yellow fins, brownish-black bar through eye, and a large ovate spot on soft dorsal fin. Males have a second much smaller spot at the edge of that fin.

Range and Habitat Nova Scotia to Brazil in coastal waters, usually on hard bottoms or around pilings and seawalls.

Comments Representative of eight species of butterflyfishes (Chaetodontidae) which occur in North America, this one ranging farther north than the others and more prone to occur in coastal waterways, harbors and inlets. All are exhibited in public aquaria.

Blue angelfish
Holacanthus bermudensis   15in (38cm)

Identification Generally yellowish tan with dorsal or anal spines blue and outer third of caudal fins yellow. Preopercle spiny. No ocellus on nape.
Range and Habitat New Jersey to Mexico in clear shallow waters usually on hard substrate.
Comments Feeds on sponges. Commonly exhibited in aquaria. Representative of seven angelfishes (Pomacanthidae) which occur in North America. All are warm-water species.

Redtail surfperch
Amphistichus rhodoterus   16in (40cm)

Identification Spinous and soft dorsal fin broadly joined. Fins red.
Body silvery to brassy with many darker bars, these often indistinct.
Range and Habitat British Columbia to California on surfy beaches.
Comments Caught by surf casters. This and the shiner perch are
representative of 19 species of surfperches, Embiotocidae, found along
the Pacific coast. All are live bearing.

Shiner perch
Cymatogaster aggregata   7in (18cm)

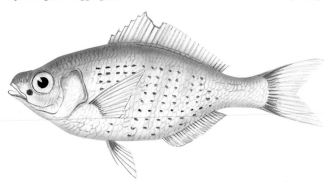

Identification Silvery with darker gray back. Rows of dark spots on
sides and three vertical yellow bars (absent in males). Males blackish
in breeding season (winter and spring).
Range and Habitat Alaska to Baja California mostly in bays and
sloughs, especially around seawalls and pilings. Enters fresh water.
Comments Caught on small hooks.

Sergeant major
Abudefduf saxatilis   7in (18cm)

Identification Yellow above, silvery to white below with five blackish bars extending to flanks.
Range and Habitat Nearly worldwide, from the Scotian Shelf southward. In coastal areas around seawalls, pilings, rocky grooves and on reefs. Also pelagic in sargassum weed.
Comments Commonly exhibited in aquaria. Eggs laid on hard surface and safeguarded by male. This and garibaldi represent 16 species of the Family Pomacentridae, most of which are restricted to warm water. All swim primarily by flapping the pectoral fins.

Garibaldi
Hypsipops rubicundus   14in (36cm)

Identification Adults entirely bright orange. Young have bluish spots of varying sizes, blue edges to the fins, and a dark nape.
Range and Habitat California and Baja California in rocky areas.
Comments Easily seen from shore. Protected in California. Commonly exhibited in aquaria.

Striped mullet
Mugil cephalus   36in (91cm)

Identification Elongate, rounded body; silvery with dark stripes on side. Spinous dorsal small, widely separated from soft dorsal. Dorsal and anal fins unscaled.
Range and Habitat Nearly worldwide in warm waters, from southeastern Canada and California southward. In large schools in coastal waters, including bays and estuaries and entering fresh water.
Comments An important commercial species, under-utilized in North America. Excellent fresh and smoked.

Great barracuda
Sphyraena barracuda   6½ft (2m)

Identification Snout long, mouth large with prominent teeth. Dorsal fins widely separate. Black blotches on side and usually has many dark bars on upper side.
Range and Habitat Nearly worldwide in warm waters, both pelagic and coastal; those in coastal waters usually territorial.
Comments A potentially dangerous fish to be viewed with caution by divers. It tends to be very curious. Most attacks occur on those wearing bright objects (especially if the water is not clear), or carrying speared fish. This is the largest of five barracudas, Family Sphyraenidae, occurring in North America. The flesh is ciguatoxic. World record 83lbs (37.6kg) but known to reach 106lbs (48kg).

Hogfish
Lachnolaimus maximus   36in (91cm)

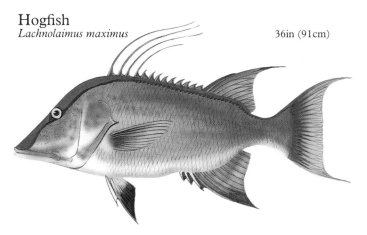

Identification Snout long, forehead concave, body deep. Reddish with dark spot at base of soft dorsal. Males with region from tip of head to dorsal fin darker purplish-brown and with first three dorsal spines very long, largely separate.
Range and Habitat North Carolina to South America in coastal waters. Juveniles in inshore grass beds.
Comments Very easily speared and overfished. Sold as snapper or hog snapper but large fish are often ciguatoxic. Reportedly to 45lbs (20kg). World record sports catch 19lb 8oz (8.8kg).

Tautog
Tautoga onitus   36in (91cm)

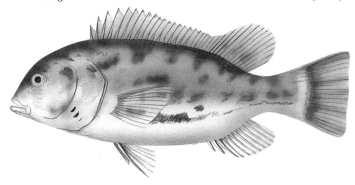

Identification Rounded body profile, males have large rubbery lips and white chin, with white area on midside. Otherwise gray with blackish network of blotches.
Range and Habitat Nova Scotia to South Carolina on hard irregular bottom and entering harbors around piers, pilings, seawalls and waters.
Comments Commonly caught by anglers. Taken commercially in pots and traps. Also speared and trawled. World record 24lbs (10.9kg).

Cunner
Tautogolabrus adspersus   15in (38cm)

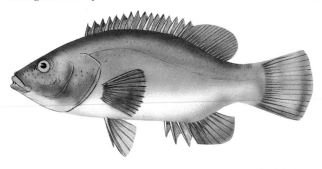

Identification Snout pointed, olive-gray to brown overall with the blotches tending to form rather obscure bars. Sometimes with black spot at front of dorsal fin.
Range and Habitat Newfoundland to Virginia along rocky shores and in harbors around seawalls, piers, ship hulls, and pilings.
Comments Not highly regarded by anglers but caught in large numbers and good pan-fried.

California sheephead
Semicossoyphus pulcher   36in (91cm)

Identification Distinctive colors; males black-red-black with white chin, females pale red to pink with white chin, and juvenile bright red with white lateral stripe and black spots in fins.
Range and Habitat California to northwestern Mexico on rocky bottom and in kelp beds from near surface to 180ft (55m).
Comments This species reverses sex, changing to male with age and growth. Commonly speared but greatly overfished and in need of protection. Reaches 36lbs (16kg). Said to be good eating. Some 24 wrasses, Family Labridae, occur in North America, most in Atlantic. The preceding four species are among the larger and better known.

Rainbow parrotfish
Scarus guacamaia   4ft (1.2m)

Identification Bluish-green, parrot-like jaws. Body pale orangish brown in front and on caudal fin, greenish on rear half of body. Smaller fish with scales greenish with tan bands.
Range and Habitat Florida to Argentina in shallow waters on rocky and coralline substrates. Caught from bridges and eaten, but flesh soft.
Comments All parrotfish swim by flapping pectoral fins. This is one of the larger of the 14 parrotfishes, Family Scaridae, which occur in warm and tropical waters of the southeastern USA.

Northern ronquil
Ronquilus jordani

7in (18cm)

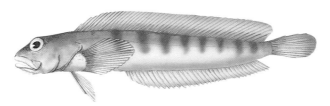

Identification Long, high, dorsal fin without spines. Caudal fin rounded. Lateral line not arched, placed rather high on side. Body slender, generally olive brown.
Range and Habitat Alaska to California on rocky bottom from shallow water, especially in north to 540ft (165m).
Comments One of five ronquils, Family Bathymasteridae, along Pacific coast.

Fish doctor
Gymnelus viridis

10in (25cm)

Identification Long tapering body, the dorsal, caudal and anal fins joined. Mouth terminal. Pale brownish, usually plain but sometimes with faint bars. Gill opening a slit. No pelvic fins.
Range and Habitat Circumpolar, southward on our coast to Nova Scotia and Alaska.
Comments One of the most northerly distributed of all fishes. This and the ocean pout are two of 34 species of eelpouts, Family Zoarcidae, known from North America.

Ocean pout
Macrozoarces americanus 42in (1.1m)

Identification Variously yellowish to reddish brown but always with dark brown blotching on side. Dorsal fin has posterior rays abruptly shorter, as if cut off.
Range and Habitat Southern Labrador to Virginia from intertidal areas (in north to 600ft (183m), mostly on hard substrate.
Comments Used for fish meal. Has been harvested commercially and flesh white and flaky. Reaches 12lbs (5.4kg).

Monkeyface prickleback
Cebidichthys violaceus 30in (76cm)

Identification Very elongate with long dorsal and anal fin and a small rounded caudal fin. Pelvic fins absent. White-edged dark bars radiate from eye. Large fleshy bump on top of head in adults.
Range and Habitat Oregon to Baja California on rocky coasts in tide pools and subtidal areas.
Comments Caught by pole anglers who poke their gear into holes and crevices in surge channels. Good eating. To at least 6lbs (2.7kg).

Slender cockscomb
Anoplarchus insignis

4¾in (12cm)

Identification Long, slender body with fleshy ridge on top of head from snout to occiput. No pelvic fins. Dark brown with ladder pattern on back, and mottled sides.
Range and Habitat Alaska to California on rocky subtidal areas.
Comments Stranded in tidepools at low-tide, often in the seaweed hanging above the water line.

Daubed shanny
Lumpenus maculatus

7in (18cm)

Identification Dorsal fin spiny, a long arch, highest above anus. Body yellowish tan with dark brown blotching.
Range and Habitat Arctic Ocean south to Massachusetts and Washington, from intertidal zone (in Atlantic part of range) to about 1650ft (503m).
Comments A common forage fish not used by man. The preceding three species are typical of 32 pricklebacks, Family Stichaeidae, all cold water, occurring in North America.

Giant wrymouth
Cryptacanthodes giganteus   46in (1.2m)

Identification Upturned mouth. Three rows of dark brown spots along side. No pelvic fins. Dorsal fin entirely spinous. Very elongate body, scaled posteriorly.
Range and Habitat Alaska to California on muddy bottom from below the low-tide line to 420ft (128m).
Comments This and wrymouth belong to the Cryptacanthodidae, a small family of coldwater fishes, three of which occur in North America.

Wrymouth
Cryptacanthodes maculatus   36in (91cm)

Identification Similar to giant wrymouth but dorsal fin heavily spotted and body without scales.
Range and Habitat Labrador to New Jersey in muddy bottom from interstitial zone to 33ft (10m).
Comments A burrowing species, caught by anglers but not used for food.

Penpoint gunnel
Apodichthys flavidus

18in (46cm)

Identification Eel-like body, uniformly red, yellow-green, or brown with dark bar below eye and with row of white (or dark) spots along side and on dorsal and anal fin.
Range and Habitat Alaska to California, mainly in tidepools in mats of attached algae.
Comments A winter spawner, easily caught and frequently seen in public aquaria and "living tidepool" exhibits.

Rock gunnel
Pholis gunnellus

12in (30cm)

Identification Blackish streak from corner of mouth through eye to top of head and then curving rearward. Body reddish to yellowish-brown, unpatterned. Row of black spots along base of dorsal fin.
Range and Habitat North Atlantic coast from Labrador to Delaware, mostly in the interstitial area on rocky shores usually in association with algae, but extending into deeper water to 600ft (183m).
Comments A minor forage species. Eleven gunnels (Pholidae) occur in cold water in North America of which the penpoint gunnel and this species are representative.

Northern wolffish
Anarhichas denticulatus   6ft (1.8m)

Identification Head large with large mouth and powerful canine teeth. Body deep forward but tapering toward caudal fin. Long-based dorsal and anal fins. Pelvic fins absent.
Range and Habitat North Atlantic coast from Labrador to New Jersey on rough, hard bottom between 50–500ft (15–150m).
Comments A sport fish. World record 37lb 7oz (17kg). Texture of flesh poor, jelly-like, so catches are discarded.

Atlantic wolffish
Anarhichas lupus   5ft (1.5m)

Identification Rather dark gray overall with dark bars across dorsal fin and body (except below).
Range and Habitat North Atlantic coast from Labrador to New Jersey.
Comments A food and sport fish, commercially harvested in Greenland and Gulf of Maine. World record 52lbs (23.6kg).

Spotted wolffish
Anarhichas minor

6ft (1.8m)

Identification Many blackish spots on head, body and fins. Otherwise similar to other wolffishes.
Range and Habitat North Atlantic coast from western Greenland along the Scotian Shelf to Massachusetts, usually deeper than 300ft (91m).
Comments A food and sport fish, harvested commercially, usually by long lines, its skin used for leather.

Wolf-eel
Anarrhichthys ocellatus

8ft (2.4m)

juvenile

Identification Eel-like fish. Gray with clusters of black spots, often white-ringed, on dorsal fin and back. Head blunt with large mouth and tusk-like teeth in front, molars in back. No pelvic fins.
Range and Habitat North Pacific coast from Alaska to California along rocky shores from intertidal to 740ft (225m).
Comments An incidental sport fish. Said to be good eating. Eggs laid in mass and guarded by female.

Prowfish
Zaproa silenus 34½in (88cm)

Identification Deep but long, compressed body. Forehead steep, rounded. Long broad dorsal and anal fins. No pelvic fins. Olive-gray to brown, paler below with darker spotting and radiating lines around rear part of eye. Large white pores on head and shoulder. Caudal fin truncate.
Range and Habitat North Pacific coast from Alaska to California on bottom, usually between 100–600ft (30–183m).
Comments Only species in the Family Zaproidae.

Yellowhead jawfish
Opistognathus aurifrons 4in (10cm)

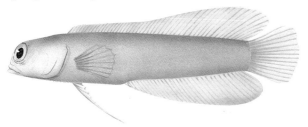

Identification Body elongate, head blunt, forehead rounded and steep. Eyes large. Yellow anteriorly, tan to pale blue posteriorly. Caudal fin rounded. Mouth large.
Range and Habitat Florida to South America on white calcareous sand which males excavate in clear shallow waters, often around coral reefs.
Comments Hovers above burrows. Egg balls brooded orally by males. A popular fish with marine aquarists. Representative of eight Atlantic species of the Family Opistognathidae, all in tropical Atlantic waters.

Northern stargazer
Astroscopus guttatus   22in (56cm)

Identification Small, separate, blackish spinous dorsal fin. Whitish
behind small eyes, spots on dark brownish body. Electric organ on top
of head. Mouth opens upward. Lips fringed.
Range and Habitat New York to North Carolina in clear shallow
water over open sand.
Comments Produces electricity. A lurking species, one of five of the
Family Uranoscopidae in North American waters, this being the most
northern. Reaches 20lbs (9.1kg).

Striped kelpfish
Gibbonsia metzi   9½in (24cm)

Identification Dorsal fin notched anteriorly, with small soft-rayed
portion distinctly higher at rear. Usually brownish but varies to
greenish or reddish.
Range and Habitat British Columbia to Baja California in seaweed
along rocky shore in intertidal and subtidal zones, often in kelp beds.
Comments Easily caught in tidepools under algal mats and exhibited
in aquaria.

Giant kelpfish
Heterostichus rostratus   24in (61cm)

Identification Caudal fin shallowly forked, green to brown; in brown phase often barred or mottled. Long, sloping head, its upper profile slightly concave.
Range and Habitat British Columbia to Baja California on rocky coasts along seaweed and kelp beds from shore to 130ft (39m).
Comments Caught by anglers or speared and eaten, but a marginal food and sport fish. Clinids, Family Clinidae, are divided into several families by some ichthyologists. Some 42 species occur in North American waters, mostly in the tropical Atlantic. The northern stargazer and striped kelpfish represent colder water Pacific forms.

Striped blenny
Chasmodes bosquianus   4in (10cm)

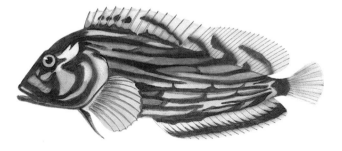

Identification Body without scales. Spinous and soft dorsal fin fully united, without notch. Head pointed. Body gray to tan with dark, wavy stripes.
Range and Habitat New York to northern Gulf of Mexico but absent from most of Florida. On hard bottom, usually near water's edge, around oysters, mussels, or barnacles. In north in deeper water in winter months.
Comments This and feather blenny represent the Blennidae, of which 18 species occur in North American warm waters. Florida blenny, *C. saburrae*, replaces this species in Florida.

Feather blenny
Hypsoblennius hentz   4in (10cm)

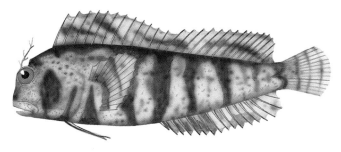

Identification Body tan to gray, somewhat mottled, with five dark bands, often poorly defined. Dorsal fin united but somewhat notched. Forehead steep. High feathery cirrus along eye.
Range and Habitat Nova Scotia to Texas on rocky shores.
Comments Especially common on oyster reefs.

American sand lance
Ammodytes americanus   10in (25cm)

Identification Elongate, with sharply pointed snout, and long-rayed dorsal fin. Caudal forked. No pelvic fins. Scales form diagonal "plates" on body.
Range and Habitat Arctic coast of eastern Canada to North Carolina from intertidal regions to offshore banks.
Comments A valuable forage fish, also fished commercially for processing into fish meal and oil. Massive die-offs are known. Fast-growing larvae are abundant and may be important predators on the larvae of other important fishes. Two other species of the Family Ammodytidae occur in our waters. This species is very similar to the European species.

Arrow goby
Clevelandia ios

2in (5cm)

Identification Spinous and soft dorsal fins separated. Very large mouth, the gape extending behind eye. Tan or grayish with small rows of black spots on fins.
Range and Habitat British Columbia to Baja California in estuaries, bays, tidal creeks, and sloughs on muddy bottom. Enters fresh water.
Comments The Family Gobiidae, of which this and the neon goby are representative, is one of the two largest families of fishes with more than 2000 species, of which 72 occur on North American coasts, mostly in warm water.

Neon goby
Gobiosoma oceanops

2in (5cm)

Identification Bright blue stripe from in front of eye to caudal fin, black above and below stripe. Belly white.
Range and Habitat Southern Florida and Texas to Central America, mostly on brain coral but may occur on rocky shores when water is clear.
Comments A very popular aquarium fish and commercially important in this regard. One of many gobies that remove ectoparasites from other fishes.

Ocean surgeon
Acanthurus bahianus   12in (30cm)

Identification Spine on side of caudal peduncle, opening outward from the front, like a pocket-knife. Usually tan with polar ring at base of tail and blue and orange stripes in dorsal fins. Caudal fins rather lunate.
Range and Habitat Massachusetts to Brazil, in schools in shallow coastal waters and around reefs.
Comments Feeds on algae. Commonly exhibited in aquaria. Caudal spine can cause a wound if the fish is handled carelessly.

Louvar
Luvarus imperialis

6ft (1.8m)

Identification Silvery with bright red fins, a deeply forked caudal fin and a tiny mouth. Deep groove above eye. Anus under pectoral fin and covered by pelvic flap. Sometimes with dark spots. Eye small, low on head.

Range and Habitat Worldwide in cold waters; on coasts from Connecticut to Gulf of Mexico and Oregon to California. Oceanic, probably mesopelagic in 600–2000ft (183–609m).

Comments A rather bizarre fish, occasionally washing ashore or found at the surface at which time it attracts much attention. Related to the surgeonfishes.

Escolar
Lepidocybium flavorbrunneum 6ft (1.8m)

Identification Entirely dark brown with a purplish cast. Skin smooth. Five to six finlets behind soft dorsal and four behind anal fin. Spinous dorsal very low, not easily seen.
Range and Habitat Worldwide; from Nova Scotia to Gulf of Mexico and off California. Pelagic and mesopelagic fish 180–600ft (55–183m).
Comments Caught on long lines. Harvested in some areas but flesh very oily. To 100lbs (45kg).

Oilfish
Ruvettus pretiosus 6ft (1.8m)

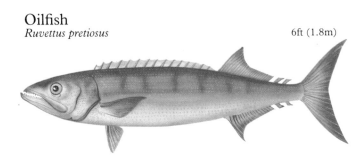

Identification Rich dark brown, the skin spiny and rough. Eye green. Only two finlets behind dorsal and anal fin. Spinous dorsal low, but easily seen.
Range and Habitat Worldwide. From Newfoundland and California southward, on or above rough bottom on the deep shelf and upper slope to 2000ft (610m).
Comments Harvested commercially in some areas but fish very oily and spoils rapidly. Caught by anglers with "deep" rigs. World record 139lb 15oz (63.5kg).

Atlantic cutlassfish
Trichiurus lepturus   5ft (1.5m)

Identification Body very long, tapering to a point and compressed.
No caudal fin. No pelvic fins. Silvery. Mouth large with strong fang-
like teeth.
Range and Habitat Massachusetts to Argentina from coastal bays,
harbors, inlets to open coastal waters and banks and even slope
waters.
Comments Commonly caught by anglers. Incursions into bays
seems periodic and often in great numbers, evoking public interest.
Pacific cutlassfish, *T. nitens*, found off California, is questionably
distinct.

Wahoo
Acanthocybium solandri   7ft (2.1m)

Identification Snout long, beak-like, dark blue above, white below
with many dark wavy bars across side.
Range and Habitat Nearly worldwide in tropical waters; from New
Jersey southward. Oceanic and pelagic, coming into reefs and shore
waters where clear condition exist.
Comments A premier sport fish, world record 149lbs (67.6kg), but
known to reach 183lbs (83kg). A powerful swimmer noted for its
strong rushes with the bait and the ability to strip line.

Frigate mackerel
Auxis thazard

20in (51cm)

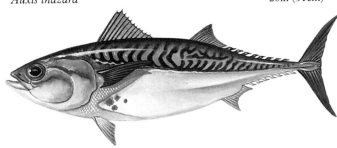

Identification A small tuna with bullet-like body, a gap between the dorsal fins and with back crossed by dark diagonal bars. Area below pectoral fin usually with several blackish spots. Corselet on front of body, the rear part without scales.
Range and Habitat Worldwide in tropics, in North America only from Florida and California. Oceanic, but taken near shore in Florida.
Comments A food and sport fish. Very similar bullet mackerel, *A. ochei*, occurs from the Scotian Shelf to the Carolinas and also off Florida. The bars on its back are aligned vertically. Both often mistaken for little tunny.

Little tunny
Euthynnus alletteratus

39in (1m)

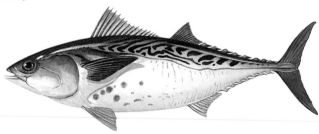

Identification Dorsal fins contiguous. Dark spots below pectoral fin. Blue above with wavy dark bars; silvery or white on sides and below. Corselet in front.
Range and Habitat Massachusetts to Brazil, also in eastern Atlantic. Pelagic but commonly occurring over the shelf near shore where clear waters exist.
Comments An important food and sport fish. Occurs in large schools. Good to eat. Used also for bait for big game fishes like marlin. World record 35lb 2oz (16kg).

Skipjack tuna
Katsuwonus pelamis

40in (1m)

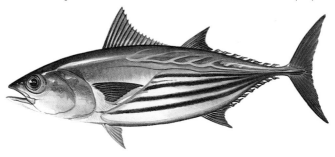

Identification Blue above, white below with long black stripes along lower half of body. No spots under pectoral fin. Corselet in front.
Range and Habitat Worldwide; from Nova Scotia and British Columbia southward.
Comments An important food and sport fish, occurring in large schools. World record 41lb 14oz (19kg) but slightly larger fish have been landed commercially.

Atlantic bonito
Sarda sarda

36in (91cm)

Identification Bluish or greenish above with many diagonal black stripes sloping up and to the rear across back. White below. Corselet present but rear of body also scaled.
Range and Habitat Both sides of Atlantic; from Gulf of St Lawrence southward. Oceanic but coming into shallow waters and offshore banks and in Canadian waters.
Comments Food and sport fish. World record 18lb 4oz (82kg).

Chub mackerel
Scomber japonicus   20in (51cm)

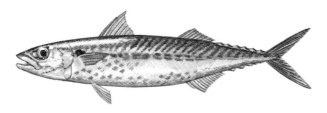

Identification No corselet, body completely scaled. Usually greenish above with many wavy, black but nearly vertical bars. White or silvery below. Usually with black spots along midside.
Range and Habitat Worldwide; near coast from Gulf of St Lawrence and Alaska southward. Pelagic but commonly entering shallow coastal waters where waters are cool.
Comments A food and sport fish. World record 4lb 12oz (2.2kg).

Atlantic mackerel
Scomber scombrus   22in (56cm)

Identification Bluish to greenish above with numerous nearly black vertical bars. No spots on side. Whitish below.
Range and Habitat North Atlantic coast from Labrador to North Carolina in open coastal waters. Pelagic.
Comments Food and sport fish. Occurs in large schools. Moves inshore during summer months. Catches were much larger 100 years ago. World record 2lb 2oz (1kg) but reaches 7lb 8oz (3.4kg).

King mackerel
Scomberomorus cavalla   5½ft (1.7m)

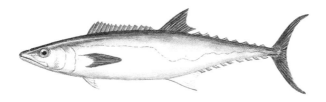

Identification Lateral line not sloping regularly but dipping sharply followed by an arch.
Range and Habitat Nova Scotia to Brazil. Adults, pelagic, offshore, the juveniles common in bays and shore waters.
Comments An important food and sport fish. World record 90lbs (40.8kg). Young are usually confused with Spanish mackerel because of large brassy spots on side.

Spanish mackerel
Scomberomorus maculatus   37in (94cm)

Identification Like king mackerel in general form, with many bronzish, brown, or golden spots on sides. Lateral line slopes downward gradually without any strong undulations.
Range and Habitat Open coastal waters and larger bays and inlets from Cape Cod to Gulf of Mexico and Cuba.
Comments An important food and sport fish, featured in seaside restaurants. World record 13lbs (5.9kg). Has disappeared from many bays due to increased turbidity and pollution. Stocks reduced.

Yellowfin tuna
Thunnus albacares 7ft (2.1m)

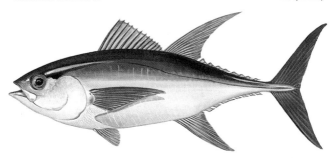

Identification Soft dorsal and anal fins and all finlets bright yellow. Yellow stripe along side. Anterior lobe of soft dorsal and anal fin become very long in large fish.
Range and Habitat Worldwide, oceanic; on coasts from Nova Scotia and California southward.
Comments Schools in open ocean. An important food and sport fish. World record 388lb 12oz (176kg). A deep diving tuna known to feed along the bottom in slope waters.

Albacore
Thunnus alalunga 4¼ft (1.3m)

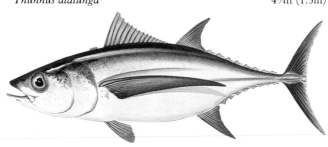

Identification Pectoral fin very long, extending back over second and third anal finlet. Body deepest under origin of second dorsal fin angled downward to snout, the dorsal profile nearly straight. Fins dark. No yellow except sometimes on dorsal finlets.
Range and Habitat Worldwide, oceanic; on coast from Nova Scotia southward, usually well offshore.
Comments The premier commercial tuna, and the most highly priced; white-fleshed and marketed as white meat as opposed to light-meat tuna. An important sport fish as well. World record 88lb 2oz (40kg) but slightly larger fish are known.

Bigeye tuna
Thunnus obesus   7¾ft (2.4m)

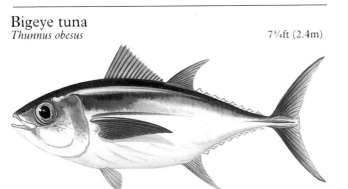

Identification Pectoral fin reaches below soft dorsal fin. Finlets
yellow but dark edged. Eye large. Snout rather blunt.
Range and Habitat Worldwide, oceanic; on coast from the
Canadian banks and Washington southward.
Comments Schools in open water. An important food and sport fish.
World record 435lbs (197kg).

Bluefin tuna
Thunnus thynnus   14ft (4.3m)

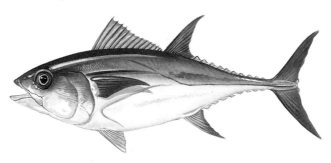

Identification Pectoral fin short, ending well ahead of soft dorsal fin.
Finlets yellow but fins dark with little if any yellow in soft dorsal and
anal fins. Eye small.
Range and Habitat Worldwide; on coast from Labrador and Alaska
southward. Pelagic but entering shore waters in northern part of
range.
Comments Very important food and sport fish. World record
1496lbs (651kg). Stocks depleted. Can maintain body temperature
well above that of surrounding water.

Swordfish
Xiphias gladius

15ft (4.5m)

Identification Upper jaw very long, flattened, sword-like, one broad keel on side of caudal peduncle. First dorsal fin rigid. No pelvic fins.
Range and Habitat Worldwide; on coast from northern Newfoundland and Oregon southward. Oceanic, basically mesopelagic, but entering surface waters in cold part of range, otherwise usually below thermocline.
Comments A premier food and sport fish. World record 1182lbs (536kg) but fish to 1300lbs (590kg) long reported.

Sailfish
Istiophorus platypterus

10¾ft (3.3m)

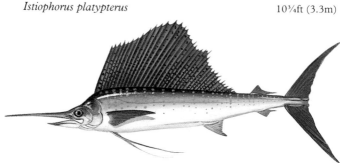

Identification Spinous dorsal fin very high, sail-like, notched behind front lobe in Pacific fish, not so in Atlantic. Nape humped. Two keels on side of caudal peduncle. Upper jaw forming a long, rounded beak.
Range and Habitat Worldwide, pelagic; on coast from New York and southern California southward.
Comments An important sport fish, harvested commercially elsewhere, the systematic status of populations in different regions unclear and there may be more than one species. World records: Atlantic 128lb 1oz (58.1kg); Pacific 221lbs (100kg).

Blue marlin
Makaira nigricans

14¾ft (4.5m)

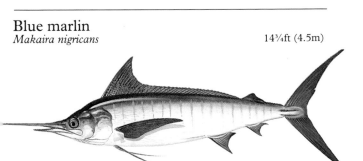

Identification Bill long, rounded in cross section. Lateral line forms chain-like pattern on side. Dark blue above, whitish below, with dark bars. Pectoral fin not rigid. Anterior lobe of spinous dorsal fin pointed.
Range and Habitat Worldwide in warm waters, oceanic, pelagic; on coast from southern Nova Scotia and California southward.
Comments The Indo-Pacific populations are regarded by some as a distinct species. One of the very largest bony fishes. A premier big game fish, also harvested commercially in other parts of the world. World records: Atlantic 1282lbs (582kg); Pacific 1376lbs (624kg) but fish in excess of 2000lbs (907kg) have been landed.

White marlin
Tetrapturus albidus

9ft (2.7m)

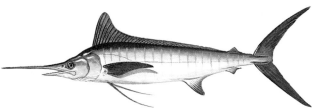

Identification Like blue marlin but anterior lobe of spinous dorsal and anal fins high and rounded or truncate, not pointed. Dark blue above, white below with blue bars in life.
Range and Habitat Atlantic Ocean, oceanic, pelagic; from Nova Scotia southward.
Comments A big game fish. World record 181lb 14oz (82.5kg). Post-spawning feeding concentrations occur during the summer off Maryland and the Mississippi Delta.

Striped marlin
Tetrapturus audax

13⅓ft (4.1m)

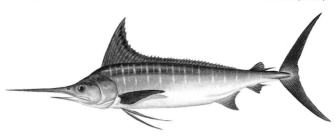

Identification Front lobe of spinous dorsal fin high but pointed, equal to depth of body. Lateral line simple and straight, not forming a chain-like pattern.
Range and Habitat Indian and Pacific oceans; on coast off California.
Comments A big game fish, harvested commercially elsewhere. World record 494lbs (224kg). Reports of fish in excess of 600lbs (272kg) are probably based on blue marlin.

Man-of-war fish
Nomeus gronovii

10in (25cm)

Identification Silvery with dark blue back and brighter blue blotches. Pelvic fin large, its inner ray broadly joined to belly.
Range and Habitat Worldwide, oceanic, pelagic; on coast from Grand Bank off Newfoundland southward.
Comments Lives in association with Portuguese man-of-war, *Physalia*, and gets blown on shore with its host during storms. These waifs do not survive. Adults may be much darker and live in deeper slope waters.

Butterfish
Peprilus triacanthus   12in (30cm)

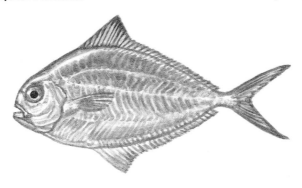

Identification Dorsal and especially the anal fin with anterior lobe only a little higher than rest of fin. Row of pores below front of dorsal fin. Silvery with dark back with many small dark spots.
Range and Habitat Newfoundland to Florida in open coastal waters.
Comments Commercially harvested, especially off the southeastern USA. Regarded as an excellent pan fish. Butterfish and man-of-war fish are representatives of the Stromateidae, an odd assemblage of fishes many of which associate with jellyfishes. Some 20 species occur along North American coasts.

Summer flounder
Paralichthys dentatus 37in (94cm)

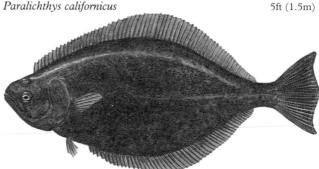

Identification Mouth large, oblique. Five ocelli in rear part of body, four in two pairs with fifth as midline in between. Other ocelli may be present. Lateral line with arch in front.

Range and Habitat New Brunswick to Florida in shallow coastal waters and bays.

Comments This, California halibut and fourspot flounder are representative of the lefteye flounders, Bothidae, of which 39 species occur on coast. All the larger species are food and sport fishes. This species reaches 26lbs (12kg); the world record sport catch is 22lb 7oz (10.2kg).

California halibut
Paralichthys californicus 5ft (1.5m)

Identification Dark olive-brown to blackish, without ocelli or well-developed pattern but may be blotched. Large mouth, rear of jaw below hind margin of eye.

Range and Habitat Washington to Baja California on rocky shores from subtidal to fairly deep water.

Comments Food and sport fish, world record 50lbs (22.7kg) but fish to 72lbs (32.7kg) reported. This species shows frequent reversal so that right-sided fish are fairly common.

Fourspot flounder
Paralichthys oblongus   16in (40cm)

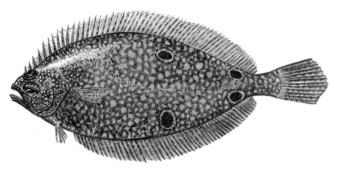

Identification Eyes very large and close together. Two pairs of dark ocellated spots. Lateral line arched in front.
Range and Habitat New Brunswick to Florida, from shallow coastal waters and bays and inlets in north to deep shelf and slope waters in south.
Comments A food and sport fish mostly marketed locally.

Rex sole
Errex zachirus   23in (58cm)

Identification Right-eyed flounder. Mouth small, ending in front of eye. Eyes large. Lateral line straight. Pectoral fin (eyed side) blackish, longer than head.
Range and Habitat Bering Sea to Baja California on soft bottom from 60ft (18.3m) to slope waters.
Comments Important food fish. This and the following eight species are all right-eyed flounder, Pleuronectidae, of which 31 species, many of them of considerable importance, occur in North American coastal waters.

Witch flounder
Glyptocephalus cynoglossus

31in (78cm)

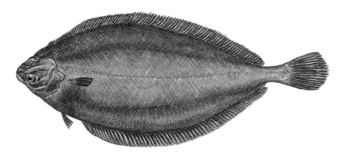

Identification Lateral line straight. Pectoral fin shorter than head. Large pits on head on blind side. Uniformly dark brown.
Range and Habitat North Atlantic coast from Labrador to North Carolina, usually in fairly deep waters 165-950ft (50-289m). To 11lbs (5kg).
Comments An important commercial species often marketed as "fillets of sole."

American plaice
Hippoglossoides platessoides

32in (81cm)

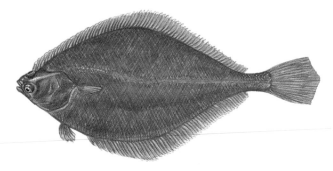

Identification Large mouth reaches below rear edge of eye. Lateral line slightly higher in front but not arched. Dark brown, sometimes reddish.
Range and Habitat North Atlantic coast from Labrador to Rhode Island primarily on the outer shelf and upper slope 120-2300ft (36-701m).
Comments A very important commercial species accounting for about half of all flatfish landings in Canada. Of lesser importance in USA.

Atlantic halibut
Hippoglossus hippoglossus   8ft (2.4m)

Identification Lateral line with distinct arch in front. Caudal fin very shallowly forked.
Range and Habitat North Atlantic coast from Labrador to Virginia.
Comments This and Pacific halibut are the largest of all flatfishes. An important food and sport fish. The world record is 255lb 4oz (116kg) but known to reach 800lbs (317kg).

Pacific halibut
Hippoglossus stenolepis   8¾ft (2.7m)

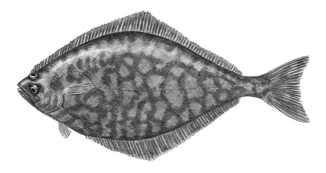

Identification Generally very dark brown on eyed side, somewhat mottled. Lateral line arched in front. Edge of caudal fin shallowly concave.
Range and Habitat North Pacific, from Bering Sea to California from near shore to deep water (3600ft (1097m).
Comments Important commercial and sport fish. World record 356lb 8oz (162kg). The fishery is now carefully regulated. Most are caught by long lines.

Winter flounder
Pleuronectes americanus   25in (64cm)

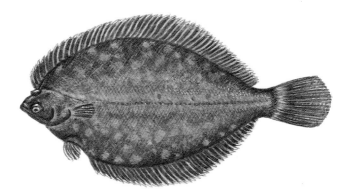

Identification Mouth small. Lateral line straight. Generally dark brown on eyed side, often mottled. Caudal fin rounded.
Range and Habitat Labrador to Georgia in shore waters, bays and inlets, usually in less than 130ft (40m).
Comments Harvested commercially, usually as a by-catch of other fisheries. Also caught by anglers; world record 4lb 3oz (1.9kg).

Rock sole
Pleuronectes bilineatus

24in (61cm)

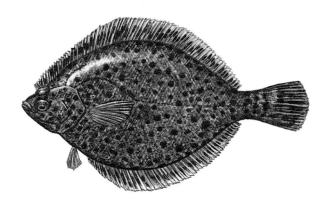

Identification Lateral line arched in front and with a separate branch in front extending under dorsal fin. Brown to gray, usually mottled.
Range and Habitat North Pacific coast from Bering Sea to California from shallow water to 1200ft (366m).
Comments An important food fish, the largest landings being in Canada.

Yellowtail flounder
Pleuronectes ferrugineus   25in (64cm)

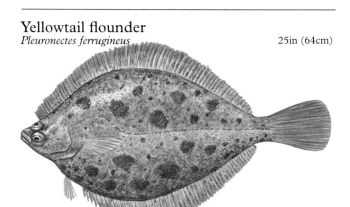

Identification Eyed side rusty brown, usually distinctly spotted.
Yellow on blind side of fins and caudal peduncle. Mouth small.
Lateral line arched.
Range and Habitat Labrador to Chesapeake Bay on soft bottom
and on banks mostly between 120-300ft (36-91m).
Comments A commercial food fish but stocks have declined. Sold
fresh or frozen.

C-O sole
Pleuronichthys coenosus   14in (36cm)

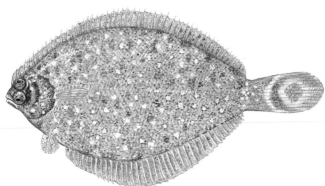

Identification Deep-bodied, lateral line straight with dorsal branch
below base of dorsal fin. Reversed, blackish "C-O" pattern on caudal
fin. Generally dark brown on eyed side, mottled.
Range and Habitat Alaska to Baja California from shallow waters to
slope waters (1150ft (350m)).
Comments A food and sport fish to minor importance. Skin is tough
and processing is difficult.

Queen triggerfish
Balistes vetula

24in (61cm)

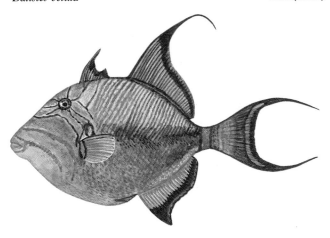

Identification Long stout dorsal spine with two smaller spines behind it serving to "lock" it in place. Body generally dark bluish-gray but underside, head and clust yellow or orangish. Yellow lines radiate from eye, two blue lines across back. Soft dorsal and caudal lobes with filamentous ray.

Range and Habitat Atlantic coast from Nova Scotia southward in shallow coastal water including bays and inlets.

Comments Exhibited in public aquaria. Occasionally caught by anglers. World record 12lbs (5.4kg). Eighteen species of the leather jacket family, Balistidae, to which both triggerfishes and filefishes belong, occur in North American waters.

Fringed filefish
Monacanthus ciliatus

8in (20cm)

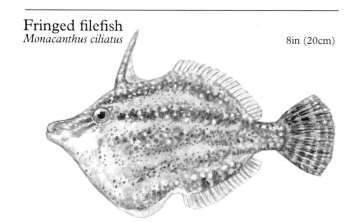

Identification Color varies, usually green or various shades of brown. Upper head profile concave. Large fleshy flap on belly, usually bordered by black with a yellow margin. Side often dark striped. Mouth small.
Range and Habitat Atlantic coast from Newfoundland southward. Common in seagrass beds in coastal waters, including bays and inlets, but also in the floating sargassum community.
Comments Easily netted and commonly exhibited in aquaria. Basically a warm-water species straying north in summer.

Striped burrfish
Chilomycterus schoepfi

10in (25cm)

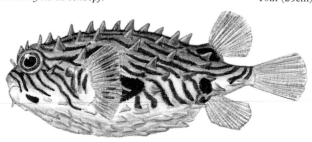

Identification Body covered with fixed sharp spines. The body striped, dark brown and yellow.
Range and Habitat Atlantic coast from Nova Scotia southward in shallow weedy areas, most common in southeastern USA.
Comments If handled carelessly, the sharp spines can cut and the powerful, parrot-like beak can cause a painful bite. Seven species of *Diodon* and *Chilomycterus* occur on Atlantic coast. They are now placed in the puffer family, Tetraodontidae, and are distinguished by their color pattern.

Balloonfish
Diodon holocanthus   20in (51cm)

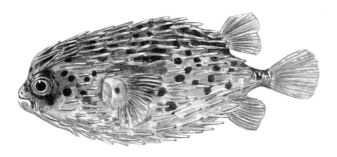

Identification Spines long, depressible. Those on top of head longer than those on body. Tan with many black spots.
Range and Habitat Worldwide; from New England and California southward.
Comments Noted for its ability to swell its body with water or air, the spines being erected by the resultant pressure. This species and the related porcupinefish, *D. hystrix*, are commonly dried, shellacked and sold as curios. Their powerful beaks enable them to crush strong mollusks like the queen conch.

Northern puffer
Sphoeroides maculatus   14in (36cm)

Identification Mottled and spotted with dark brown above, dark band between eyes. Dark brown blotches on lower side. Capable of puffing up.
Range and Habitat Newfoundland to northeastern Florida in shallow coastal waters including bays, inlets, and harbors.
Comments A locally important food fish, marketed as "sea squab," the muscles along the tail part of the body being the part used. Many puffers are toxic and great care must be taken in preparing fish to remove skin and internal organs. Eleven other species of puffers occur in North American waters.

Ocean sunfish
Mola mola

10ft (3m), reportedly larger

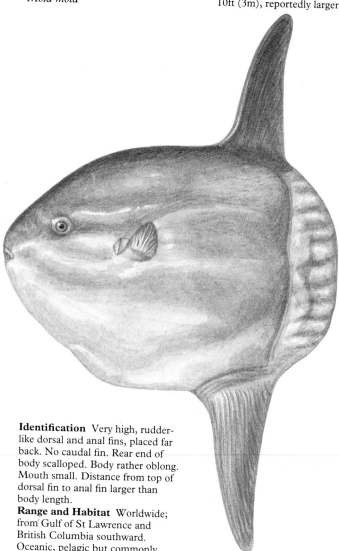

Identification Very high, rudder-like dorsal and anal fins, placed far back. No caudal fin. Rear end of body scalloped. Body rather oblong. Mouth small. Distance from top of dorsal fin to anal fin larger than body length.

Range and Habitat Worldwide; from Gulf of St Lawrence and British Columbia southward. Oceanic, pelagic but commonly coming into shallow waters, even into bays, usually when in distress.

Comments A curiosity of nature. Reported to reach 440lbs (199.5kg), and a powerful swimmer. Feeds largely on jellyfishes.

Index